Praise for Four Days to Change

Through the work and introspection during the White Men's Caucus, I've participated in one of the most impactful events in my 35-year career. Michael has captured the essence of the Caucus in his book, *Four Days to Change*. He has honed in on the essential element of this unique and enlightening experience for white men: learning to lean into our discomfort and to question our assumptions. This book will elicit a transformational experience for the reader that is essential in our increasingly diverse society.

—PAUL J. STEFFEN, Vice President, Northwestern Mutual

The W. K. Kellogg Foundation embraces differences and respects and nurtures people of all races, ethnicities, and religions as a result of our longstanding relationship with WMFDP, whose work is described in this book. Their body of work has provided the single most important factor in an organization's success, which is the ability to create an authorizing environment for learning to take place. An "authorizing environment" means that the place is completely safe at all levels, from boardrooms to bathrooms. The change garnered in four days is palpable, and its impact on lives and institutions is brought to life in *Four Days to Change*. Congratulations on providing an effective tool for the field.

—LA JUNE MONTGOMERY TABRON, President and CEO, W. K. Kellogg Foundation

Four Days to Change shows white male leaders how to strengthen their organizations by having them understand and accept their responsibility toward improving equity. It does so without shame or guilt and in a manner that encourages you and makes you proud to be a part of this work.

—LARRY O'DEA, Chief of Police, Portland, Oregon

A meaningful book that will help white men redefine their role as key leaders for inclusion and equity in the workplace.

—KEITH NOSBUSCH, CEO, Rockwell Automation

Every so often, a book comes along that enables us to see the world differently, with the inspirational power to drive one to responsible action. *Four Days to Change* is such a book. As an attendee of the White Men's Caucus, I can attest to the transformative insights Michael articulates in this easy-to-read book based upon his decades of experiential learning. I found *Four Days to Change* enormously informative and life changing, both on a personal and leadership level, as we strive to support an increasingly diverse and inclusive workforce in full partnership. A must-read for any courageous leaders ready to begin their lifelong journey of enlightenment while viewing and understanding diversity and inclusion through their white male lens.

—RICK GESING, Corporate Vice President, Worldwide Operations, Applied Materials Inc.

As a white man reading this book I felt totally engaged and fully accounted for, caught up in the transformations that were taking place in front of me. To say this is a "must-read" is to understate its importance. A real tour de force!

—THOMAS KOCHMAN, Kochman Mavrelis Associates, Inc., Coauthor, *Corporate Tribalism*, Author, *Black & White Styles in Conflict*

WMFDP has helped so many leaders rise to the opportunity to put their privilege to honorable use. In *Four Days to Change*, Michael captures the essence of an experience that transforms diversity work from "someone else's problem" into an inspiring opportunity to make the world a better place.

—MARK BURGET, Executive Vice President, The Nature Conservancy

We know from our research that to develop more inclusive workplaces, we must fully engage and empower men to serve as agents of change. In *Four Days of Change*, Michael shares powerful insights that will help any organization transform into one that leverages and embraces differences, by equipping men to lead more inclusively.

—DEBORAH GILLIS, President and CEO, Catalyst

We know we have to make race and gender visible for white men to fully engage men as allies. But how? In this valuable volume, Michael Welp compresses 20 years of facilitating that engagement into a book as deeply theoretical as it is handy and practical. Quite a feat!

—MICHAEL KIMMEL, SUNY Distinguished Professor of Sociology and Gender Studies, Executive Director, Center for the Study of Men and Masculinities, Author of more than 16 books

As a white man working in a highly masculine profession that's currently facing considerable scrutiny, *Four Days to Change* serves as a reminder of the self-reflection needed to be a leader and more active participant in creating a more connected home and community.

—PAUL SCHNELL, Chief of Police, Maplewood, Minnesota

This is one of the most profound books on culture I have ever read because it tackles the difficult problem of the culture within us that we don't see. By reviewing what happens in white men's caucuses we learn the deep cultural differences that exist between races, genders, and sexual orientations, and see how these have worked their way into western business culture and our daily life. This is a must-read for those of us who are blind to the automatic privileges we enjoy.

—EDGAR H. SCHEIN, Professor Emeritus, MIT Sloan School of Management, Author, *Humble Inquiry* and *Humble Consulting*

Four Days to Change is, more than anything else, a book about possibility. It, along with the work it represents, leaves us with hope that by honoring the human condition and shining the light of consciousness on ourselves and others, we actually have the ability to transcend the wounds that divide us from others, and even from our own true nature. Thank you for this book. Thank you even more for your work.

—HOWARD J. ROSS, Founder, Cook Ross, Inc., Author, *Everyday Bias and ReInventing Diversity*

A courageous book about the critical journey and lessons that enable white men to live and work authentically across differences.

—JUDITH H. KATZ and FREDERICK A. MILLER, The Kaleel Jamison Consulting Group, Inc., Coauthors: *Inclusion Breakthrough* and *Opening Doors to Teamwork and Collaboration*

Four Days to Change can transform your mind, your heart, and your life! Shattering the Myth of Meritocracy, this important book opens the eyes of white male leader—like me—and points us to a much more inclusive, authentic and value-creating world.

—KEVIN CASHMAN, Senior Partner, CEO and Executive Development, Korn Ferry, Author, *Leadership from the Inside Out* and *The Pause Principle*

Four Days to Change

Other Books coauthored by Michael Welp:

Diversity Partnership Tips for White Men

Diversity Partnership Tips for White Women and People of Color to Engage White Men

Eight Critical Leadership Skills Created Through Effective Diversity Partnerships

To my daughters Nina and Lydia. I hope this book will help all of us make the world a better place for you and your generation across the globe.

And to all the white men who have attended a White Men's Caucus over the past twenty years. Every caucus has felt sacred to me as I and other staff have witnessed your heartfelt learning and courageous conversations.

CONTENTS

Appendices

FOREWORD

I know what you're probably thinking: A book focused on the "needs" of white men? Oh please.

Before you put this down in frustration, I should clarify that this is a book about diversity, equality, and inclusion, and why white men *need* to see these issues as *their* issues.

It's a book about a journey that thousands have already taken with our organization to join the global effort to create equitable and sustainable organizations that bring out the best in everyone—including themselves.

In April 1990, I learned of the passing of my mentor, Harrison Simms. His death changed me, bringing into focus what would become my central pursuit for the next twenty-five years.

My relationship with Harrison began three years earlier. Having just moved to the Pacific Northwest, I received an invitation to attend a workshop led by Harrison titled "Celebrating Differences through Building Alliances" at a conference in Port Townsend, Washington. Between jobs and new to the area, I had a lot of spare time, so I went.

Little did I know that this workshop would only be the start of a long, transformative journey, one that I am still on.

An African-American man originally from the Bay Area, Harrison opened a door to a parallel universe previously unknown to me. That day in 1987, I took my first step out of the cosseted universe of inclusion, equity, privilege, and culture I had unconsciously enjoyed up until that point as a straight, white male.

Harrison had the profound ability to love people into full consciousness. When I arrived at that workshop, I might have been aware in a theoretical sense of systemic inequity and issues of difference, but I was totally blind to how those issues intersected with my own life.

Harrison awakened something deep within me, fueling my curiosity and my passion for creating change. He helped me connect the dots and really *feel* how issues of diversity and equality were as much *my* issues as they were the issues of those who struggled daily to be seen and heard in a world that largely ignored—or, worse, invalidated—their humanity and sense of self.

Harrison and I stayed in touch after that workshop and eventually began to work together. That April in 1990, he stayed as a guest in my house in Portland after we co-led a workshop on inclusion. As usual, after he left I felt like an impostor, simply in awe of Harrison's ability to change minds and hearts and convinced that I would never be able to engage people on these issues the way he did and really make a difference.

Three days later, I learned that Harrison had passed away of a heart attack at age forty-seven.

Harrison's death startled me into full aliveness. I awoke the night after learning of his passing and committed then and there to follow this path. I knew deep down that this quest for diversity and inclusion was to be my life's work.

That epiphany eventually led to a grand experiment in March 1997, when I convened and facilitated the first ever learning experience about diversity, bias, and inclusion intended solely for white men. I called it the White Men's Caucus on Eliminating Racism, Sexism, and Homophobia in Organizations. (It's a mouthful, I know.)

Over the last two decades, my colleague Michael Welp and I have had the incredible privilege of working with thousands of white men—from front-line employees to key decision makers at the tops of the company org charts—in re-examining their mindsets, shifting their behaviors, and helping them exemplify the change they wished to see in their organizations, and in their lives.

With a last name like Proudman, it took me a few years to realize that the path to becoming an energized catalyst and full partner lay in more fully discovering and embracing my own white maleness. Indeed, in becoming a *proud white man.*

Naturally, we were told repeatedly that combining the words "white men" and "diversity" was oxymoronic in the extreme. White men learning about inclusion and diversity from other white men? Impossible, ridiculous, even heresy. It was not our place, we were told, to lead or even be active partners in equality and change efforts. As white men, we were supposed to stay out of the way or, at best, let others teach us.

Thankfully, Harrison had helped me discover my voice and claim my place in this journey, and I wouldn't be deterred.

There are many reasons for this reaction, of course. Historically, white men gathering together behind closed doors has been anything but positive. For obvious reasons, the work of inclusion and equality has been ceded to members of those groups who have been consistently marginalized and oppressed. Our job as white men has been to keep our heads down and defer all questions to others. If we wanted to make change, we were expected to wait for others—be they women, people of color, or members of the LGBT community—to instruct us on what to do.

Meanwhile, we walked on eggshells, afraid of being admonished for saying the wrong thing or not doing the right thing.

Gender equality was perceived as a women's issue the same way that race was seen as a problem to be addressed by people of color. Through it all, white men have been seen as silent bystanders at best and, at worst, malicious oppressors. Either way, many white men have learned to stay away from a topic they have come to see as about everyone else *but* them.

The truth, as I learned from Harrison Simms in 1987, is that these issues are our issues as much as they are the issues of any other group of people. Without the active partnership of white man, true change retreats even farther over the horizon.

Four Days to Change is the story of how Michael and I, along with other courageous white men, have rediscovered this partnership stance with each other, with women, and with people of color.

So what's White Men's Caucus all about?

White men, thanks to their often blissful cluelessness—I was no exception—are seen by every other group as the problem. That's because we see everything that happens to us as the direct result of our individual actions. We miss the systemic patterns because they don't hinder us. We are led to believe that the path forward is for everyone to simply work hard. After all, if you can dream it, you can do it. Right?

What I and other white men don't realize—until we are shown otherwise—is the impact of systemic injustice and how, while the actions of two different people may be the same, the results can be very different based on the racial and gender identities of each one.

This is a very challenging concept for many white men, particularly working-class men. It can be misinterpreted as a bid to discount their hard work or to attribute their success solely to privilege.

Through this work, I have come to more fully understand the rage and hurt oppressed and marginalized peoples have endured over time. One of the barriers that stops white men from real growth in this area is misconstruing others' pain as their own personal fault. My work has helped me see that none of this is my fault. The truth is simply that other men and I are responsible for seeing how these systemic injustices have shaped and impacted our lives and the lives of those around us. We need to become more aware, step into our unique role of helping our white male colleagues become aware, and then partner with everyone to change what we can.

It is here that Michael and I have staked our ground: the full engagement and partnership of white men, senior business leaders in particular.

Through it all, I have learned that profound human change can begin only with deeply knowing and then loving oneself.

Four Days to Change contains our most powerful learnings and insights from running over 125 caucuses over more than two decades. This transformative work has provided our clients with a roadmap for the critical role they as white men must take to chart a sustainable course into the sea of full partnership.

Some have mocked us, others have questioned our motives, and occasionally our work has been so misconstrued as to elicit threats. What I have noticed through it all is that there is never *not* a reaction. Lead with the words "white men" and you can bet there will be passion and feeling and then, ultimately, a conversation. We at White Men as Full Diversity Partners have been engaging in that dialogue for more than twenty years now, and we are just beginning to glimpse the true path to partnership.

The amazing part is that this journey is an endless one. I recognize that the more I think I know, the more there is to learn. Staying humble and using my confusion to stay curious have helped me form partnerships I never knew could exist.

I hope in your reading of *Four Days to Change* you come to discover your own path to full partnership. In a world that seems more complex and chaotic than ever, we appreciate your efforts to make a difference. This Earth is after all but one large boat. It is up to us to learn to coexist in this vessel so we may all better enjoy the ride.

In full partnership,

Bill Proudman
Portland, Oregon

Introduction

THERE'S A PRICE TO BE PAID FOR WORKPLACE DIS-crimination—$64 billion. That amount represents the annual estimated cost of losing and replacing the more than two million American workers who leave their jobs each year due to unfairness and discrimination. (Replacing an hourly worker costs companies somewhere between $5,000 and $10,000, and it's more than ten times that amount for executives.)

Four Days to Change documents and explains the remarkable, unorthodox methods of the White Men's Caucus, developed and refined over two decades by Bill Proudman and me to address—to solve—discrimination in the workplace. Diversity is one of our greatest strengths as a nation and as a global economic leader, while discrimination has long been our Achilles' heel, both morally and economically.

Despite all the gains our society has seen since the dawn of the Civil Rights Movement, discrimination remains more common than often thought. Recent studies show that one in four women in the United States have experienced workplace sexual harassment. Fully 42 percent of gay individuals say they have experienced some form of employment discrimination at some point in their lives. An astonishing 90 percent of transgender individuals report either experiencing some form of harassment, mistreatment, or discrimination on the job, or having to take actions such as hiding their gender identity to avoid it.

Replacing workers is not the only cost of discrimination—there is also litigation. In 2010, the top ten private plaintiff employment discrimination lawsuits cost companies more than $346 million.

Beyond companies, discrimination in society costs countries as a whole as well. A study titled *The Business Case for Racial Equity* was conducted with scholars from Johns Hopkins, Brandeis, and Harvard universities. The study posits that an income gap resulting in part from racism costs the United States $1.9 trillion each year. Among the more striking findings cited are a U.S. Department of Commerce study estimating that minority purchasing power would increase from $4.3 trillion to $6.1 trillion in 2045 if income inequalities were eliminated.

Retaining a diverse employee base aids in many ways beyond savings. For example, employees are 3.5 times more likely to share new ideas under diverse leadership. This includes ideas for succeeding in today's diverse marketplace: Hispanic purchasing power is $1.3 trillion. The LGBT community represents an $830 billion market opportunity. Women represent $22 trillion.

Discrimination often isn't conscious or intentional. Recent research reveals enormous amounts of unconscious or implicit bias. For example, 88 percent of whites in the United States demonstrate an unconscious bias against blacks in studies. In one experiment, a résumé with a black-sounding name received half as many callbacks as the same résumé with a white-sounding name, even when it was sent to corporations with strong diversity reputations.

Other research shows that a black college student has the same chances of getting a job as a white high school dropout. Blacks need to complete not one but two additional levels of education just to have the same probability of getting a job as a white candidate. Meanwhile, a white male with a criminal record is 5 percent more likely to get a job than an equally qualified person of color with a clean record.

Women are almost four times more likely than men to think they have fewer opportunities to advance because of their gender—and they are twice as likely to think their gender will make it harder for them to advance in the future.

Women in the United States

- ▶ Represent 50.8 percent of the U.S. population

- ▶ Earn almost 60 percent of undergraduate degrees and 60 percent of all master's degrees

- ▶ Earn 47 percent of all law degrees and 48 percent of all medical degrees

- ▶ Earn more than 44 percent of master's degrees in business and management, including 37 percent of MBAs

- ▶ Represent 47 percent of the U.S. labor force and 59 percent of the college-educated, entry-level workforce

Despite these figures, women

- ► Represent 14.6 percent of executive officers
- ► Represent 8.1 percent of top earners
- ► Represent 4.6 percent of *Fortune* 500 CEOs
- ► Hold 16.9 percent of *Fortune* 500 board seats

When asked whether "even with equal skills and qualifications, women have much more difficulty reaching top-management positions," the gender divide was striking: 93 percent of women agreed with the statement, but just 58 percent of men agreed. Men are often unaware of the barriers women face.

A new study finds that the world economy could add trillions of dollars in growth during the next ten years if countries met best-in-region scores for improving women's participation in the labor force.

Clearly there are opportunities to address issues of inclusion and equity. Yet many organizations find these issues uncomfortable and avoid any discussion of them. People walk on eggshells around the topics. Our twenty years of experience have shown us that leaders steer clear of these tough conversations partly because they have never been taught how to have such conversations. Furthermore, the burden to raise these issues usually falls to those who are most impacted by them: people of color, women, LGBT individuals, and other victims of discrimination. Meanwhile, white men, who often feel defensive and attacked, avoid the conversations at all costs.

These same organizations struggle to find ways to grow

the tough leadership skills needed for today's world. Yet these messy diversity issues provide an ideal arena to grow leadership skills in every employee, including courage, integrating head and heart, and the ability to have difficult conversations.

One of the most difficult aspects of this path is educating white men about their own blind spots in ways that leave them passionate about diversity rather than feeling blamed and attacked. To be a sustainable proposition, the heavy lifting of educating white men needs to shift away from women, people of color, and other targets of discrimination toward *other white men*.

Our work over the past twenty years has blazed a path for this to happen. White Men's Caucus has changed the beliefs and attitudes of many white men forever. Our first White Men's Caucus was held in 1997. Three years later our colleague Jo Ann Morris joined us as another co-founder of White Men as Full Diversity Partners. At that time we added a complementary four-day learning session we call the Allies Lab that includes mixed race and gender participants. Both of these labs continue to create lifelong learning in attendees.

Catalyst's research of the impact of the White Men's Caucus and our Allies Lab has been enlightening. Melissa Korn summarized these findings in her *Wall Street Journal* blog *At Work*:

A new study of nearly 100 employees at Rockwell Automation Inc., more than 60 percent of them white males, found that just a few days of training on diversity and inclusion can dramatically change how men view their role in improving their organization on those fronts. Rockwell is a maker of factory-automation equipment.

The study, which started in 2011, tracked participants' responses to a series of questions (such as whether white men have an advantage in society) shortly before a training session run by White Men as Full Diversity Partners (a firm that offers corporate diversity training), one month after, and then again four months after the program.

The attitude shift was dramatic, says Jeanine Prime, vice president of research at Catalyst, a nonprofit organization supporting women in business, which conducted the study.

Among the most important changes, she says, is how much respondents acknowledged that white men have privileges that women and racial or ethnic minorities don't. On a scale of one to seven, where one meant "strongly disagree" and seven meant "strongly agree," participants moved from a rather neutral 4.8 to a more emphatic 5.6 just four months after the course.

Breaking through the "myth of meritocracy" is a key step in establishing a more diverse workplace, Ms. Prime says. Biases often flourish when people think there's a pure meritocracy in place, but acknowledging that certain groups have fundamental advantages allows a more honest assessment of promotion practices.

Other findings: After the program, work groups reported less workplace gossip, which can contribute to a hostile atmosphere. Participants were also observed to take a greater interest in learning about people with different perspectives and they felt more responsibility for fostering an inclusive work environment.

One specific finding was that co-workers noticed the white men listened 33 percent more often after their caucus. They increasingly used the skill of inquiry across difference—asking questions inclusively of other races and women—along with four other inclusive behaviors. Stories abound of spouses who are thrilled with this change in their husbands' behavior after only three days.

Please note that the four workshop participants in the book are composites. (In fact, caucuses almost always have at least eight participants. Usually there are sixteen to eighteen.) The stories and incidents come from different people attending different caucuses across twenty years. In addition, the caucus described in the book includes some activities from the early days that we no longer use, and excludes others that we do—the focus is on revealing the learning conversations that take place as a result of our experiential activities.

I hope that *Four Days to Change* opens a window for you into a new way of seeing and thinking about diversity, as something that can be of great benefit to you and everyone else in the workplace.

ONE

Journey to South Africa

I'M NOW IN MY TWENTIETH YEAR OF RUNNING THE White Men's Caucus. The *what?* I know it might sound like some kind of supremacist movement, but it's actually the opposite. Just wait. I'll get to that. First you should understand what launched me on my journey.

It all started in 1988, when I was twenty-six years old, sitting with my classmates at the American University in Washington DC. I was one of twenty-three students. Among the Americans were seven white men, one black man, one black woman, two Hispanic women, and nine white women. Also in the mix was an Indian woman, a white Australian woman, and a white French Canadian woman. This master's program in organization development was designed for working adults and met monthly for classes. Most of the faculty came from National Training Laboratories Institute, a social change organization that had birthed the T-group, a method of studying group dynamics, and the field of organizational development. Every weekend we had a two-hour unstructured "community time" when our task was to deal with issues in our community. One of the issues we discussed was race—a discussion I will never forget.

During one particular community time meeting, the room was still except for twitches of discomfort and quiet except for occasional moans as people around the circle were leaning forward to listen to one black woman recount her story. Amid her flowing tears and deep pain were the fragments of a childhood experience when she was with her grandmother and was denied use of a public drinking fountain, marked "For Whites Only." My heart grew heavy. I felt paralyzed as I heard this story of oppression. I knew of our country's segregated history, but it had never felt as real as it became in that moment. Why had it not been real before? I don't remember the details of her story. What I carried was the depth of her pain.

There were many moments of learning in those two years. During this same session, while the black woman shared her story, one of my white male colleagues interrupted her to tell a story about when his hair was long and he drove a motorcycle. He'd been persecuted because of his appearance, he said. Others in the room, upon hearing him equate his experience with others' tales of racism and sexism, lashed out at him in anger. But it was one of the first times I witnessed another white male discuss diversity, even though he had put his foot in his mouth. I didn't know seven years later that my life's work would become guiding white men through issues of diversity.

Toward the end of that two-year program, we were sitting in our final class on ethics. Someone turned on the TV for a news special. Nelson Mandela was just being released from prison. We watched as he walked into freedom. It was unforgettable. He'd been in prison since I was a toddler. Many of my classmates were teary eyed. We'd had many tense conversations on race, and the learning for me had been monumental. I now had a deep sense of what this meant in South Africa. The world was changing, and I yearned to be part of that change.

Five months later I learned how I would indeed be part of that change. I had previously taught at Outward Bound in Minnesota and had inquired about any openings they had in Africa or Asia. The school I most wanted to work at was in Lesotho, a landlocked independent country inside South Africa, which led programs on interracial teambuilding for miners, bank employees, and staff members at pharmaceutical companies. I'd already received a letter from neighboring Zimbabwe welcoming me to volunteer but hadn't yet heard from Lesotho. I had never sent a fax before and there was no such thing as email, but one night in July I sent a fax to Lesotho Outward Bound in Africa. I really didn't believe that the paper I was sending through the machine in rural Minnesota was actually coming out of another machine across the globe. But it must have, because at 8 a.m. the next day I found a return fax from Africa offering me a job as a group tutor. My dream had come true.

Two months later I woke up in New York City to catch a flight to Johannesburg. My heart beat faster when I saw on the front page of the *New York Times* a picture of a massacre aboard a commuter train between Johannesburg and Soweto in South Africa. I wondered what adventures and what dangers awaited me. After a long flight, we made a late-night fuel stop in The Gambia of West Africa, where I stepped off the plane in the middle of the night and noticed the extreme humidity. I hated humidity but loved adventure.

On to Lusaka, Zambia, and then Johannesburg, where Collin, the Outward Bound manager who ran the city office, took me home to the Johannesburg suburb of Florida to get some sleep. I noticed the bars on the windows and doors of his house, and it reminded me of the train massacre story in the *New York Times*.

The next day we drove six hours to the base camp in Lesotho. It was my first time riding on the left side of the road, and I was struck by how much life was the same and how much it was different from back home. The countryside was beautiful. I met my fellow instructors and local staff, who welcomed me from across the world. Four of the instructors were black men from Lesotho; two of them were former Peace Corps language instructors. The others were expatriates: a Canadian woman, a British female doctor, an older British man who was a lifelong Outward Bound staffer, and two women on a gap year after high school—a British South African and an Italian. Three days later I would lead my first course.

The instructor I worked with first was Nthabeleng Zulu, a skinny man, five foot eight, who was a former pilot and sometimes wore a white sailor's cap. We spent several days planning before the rest of our group rolled into the parking lot. The students were workers from different South African corporations.

We were working with Hippo Quarries, a rock quarry company. There were two white foremen and six black workers, ranging in age from twenty-eight to forty-eight. Like all of the mining groups I would work with, the whites and the blacks worked shifts together but never ate meals at the same table, never slept in the same dorm rooms, and never drank beer together. But that was all about to change.

The black men spoke Sepedi, and they could understand the Sesotho spoken by my co-instructor Nthabeleng. I gave my opening talk in English, and it was repeated by Nthabeleng in Sesotho.

"Today we're going to learn what it really means to be a team," I said. Most of them were aware of the unspoken reason they'd been sent here.

Within ten minutes we had them doing tasks that broke barriers. The first one was to cross a swampy pond, eight feet across, that had only two parallel logs across it, a few feet apart. They were given several boards to place between the logs to stand on, and soon they were huddled together holding themselves tight so no one would fall into the green muck. That experience of supporting each other would be repeated continually over the next week, whether while climbing a ten-foot wall, belaying each other up rocky inclines, or rappelling down a fifty-foot cliff. The first night of our discussion, all of the men expressed a strong desire to work together to bridge black and white. The conversation was incredibly heartfelt, perhaps broken open by the connectedness the group already felt in the first hours of team activities.

Because most blacks and whites in South Africa had never had a beer together, this was the only Outward Bound school in the world that served beer for everyone an hour before dinner. I enjoyed that, as did the others.

One forty-eight-year-old black man, Daniel, was amazed. "All these years I never see black and white together drinking from the same mug," he marveled.

Many of the normal activities of the week—eating together, sleeping in the same room, and sharing water bottles—were brand-new experiences in the lives of these men.

It was the overnight expeditions into the surrounding countryside that would take me into deeper connections with my students and our surroundings. In the following days, we hiked through the village beyond the base camp. Local kids would run up to us—a group of white and black men with strange backpacks—in delight and curiosity.

In this village were some of the poorest people in the world, who also seemed to be some of the happiest. This was apparent when we camped in the caves high above the valleys near the ridgeline of the surrounding mountains. Below us the landscape was all open grassy fields and rolling hills, with very few trees. As the incredibly bright stars shone, we could see the campfires and hear the villagers singing, laughing, and dancing all night long. The sound of deep levels of happiness was both comforting and so energizing, it was hard to fall asleep. Eventually the roosters would announce the morning. Sometimes it was not until then that I would realize the singing had stopped.

The teamwork came so naturally that I had to remind myself how radical it was for this group to collaborate across race. One evening I was hooking up a climbing harness to a zip wire on a black worker named Godfrey.

I asked him, "Do you vote?"

"No. Voting is for white people," he said.

I realized that my question had been pretty stupid, considering I'd already known the answer. I guess I asked because my heart simply didn't want to believe it. I've never forgotten that moment. Till then, I hadn't really felt the depth of the divide. How much, as a white American, I'd taken equality for granted.

I instructed ten, week-long courses in those nine months. It was healing for the students. And for me. Whether they were white or black, they had to overcome some strong social forces. One white miner told the group his wife warned him, "If you sleep in the same room with a black man I will divorce you." We all agreed not to tell her that he did.

It was only seven months since Nelson Mandela had walked out of prison, after all. For one course, employees sent their kids to learn to get along with each other. One white girl told us what her mom said: "If you eat out of the same pot as blacks you will get sick." Prejudice ran deep, so transformations would have to go deep as well.

At the end of yet another course, a black miner named Fruitman said to me: "I'm going to be a changed man from now on, and I'm going to accept everybody as my brother and sister."

One white miner said he felt betrayed by his country; his whole life he was told things that were not true. He and other white men talked about being sent to summer camps as children, where they were taught the justification for apartheid. Whites and blacks had come to believe they were so different from each other. But in our courses, they discovered their sameness.

As Larry, one older white miner, said: "I've learned that humans are humans. I've come to see how the youth of today are going to blend."

Not everyone was as ready to change their attitudes.

Some of the white men were combative, quick to point out to me that Americans didn't get things perfect regarding race. They resented any possibility that I might be there to sermonize to them. But I did not want to or need to; their own interactions and experiences changed them more than any words I could say.

At first in my nine months there I connected more with the men of color, who would often sing and dance around the campfire in spontaneous improvisation. It took a bit longer for me to realize how much I had in common with the white men. Gradually I looked into their eyes and saw myself. By the end of those nine months I realized I needed to come back to the United States to work with people like me—other white men. I felt compelled to do it. My most important work would be with my own group, white men in the United States. And since that time twenty-five years ago, that is what my life has been about. Ironically, my work has circled back recently to include white men all around the globe.

A few years ago, I was moved to write a letter to Mandela. In it, I said,

> You showed that love is the most powerful approach to drive any change. Witnessing the change happening before me while in your country was like witnessing a fairy tale. And with the same approach of love, I now witness white men from all over the United States growing the awareness and heart strength to engage their white male colleagues in creating truly inclusive organizations and communities. Many of the white men I work with say their experience addressing diversity with other white men is life changing. One reason is that my heart carries the same thread of love which you passed onto the white men in South Africa.

This is the story of my journey and the lessons of scores of white men from around the United States and the world who have attended the White Men's Caucus. If we are to survive as a species and face today's challenges within the global community, we must do our part to adapt. We owe it to ourselves, to everyone's sons and daughters, and to our home planet Earth.

Along with stories and learning, I share the Twelve Radical Thought Habits, or new mindsets, which white men must use in an increasingly diverse world. In addition, these mindsets are critical to democracy worldwide. I also lay out the Eight Critical Leadership Skills that support these mindsets that are key not only to the workplace but to all contexts of life.

My hope is that by illuminating some of the treasures these men have found on this journey of reflection on being white, male, and mostly heterosexual, more of us will take this voyage for the benefit of others and ourselves.

TWO

Into the Darkness

IT WAS SEPTEMBER OF 1997 AND I WAS SITTING ON A bench in a hotel lobby in Chicago along with another ex–Outward Bound instructor named Bill Proudman. Bill is a large, muscular guy with disheveled hair and a short, rough beard who loves chopping wood and is an extrovert. We had met through his brother Steve, who had brought us together every September to help run a Chicago Outward Bound Center program for University of Chicago's new MBA students. Bill had been on a similar path as me, passionately exploring diversity, and had come to a similar conclusion about the need to engage white men in a new way. We were about to blaze a new trail forward as we sat in the lobby sharing recent discoveries.

My dissertation, written the previous spring, explored the lives of eight white men who were known as strong advocates of diversity. My motivation was selfish; I wanted to learn from them what my path forward might be. My biggest finding was that white men learn virtually everything about diversity from white women and people of color. Thus, white women and people of color often carry an enormous burden—educating white men. Our most important role, as white men, had to be teaching other white men. But there was something else that really bugged me about my findings. Those white male advocates began resenting other white men; they didn't like the white male part of themselves. The problems white men have aren't just with women and minorities but with themselves and each other. The most important shift for white men had to be learning to engage with each other—and with their own white maleness—from a place of love.

Now, as we sat together, Bill seemed excited about something.

"Something extraordinary has happened," he said.

He then began to tell me about a gathering he'd held called the White Men's Caucus. A few months earlier, he'd gathered every white man he could, including his father, at a bed and breakfast near Mount Adams in Washington State.

"Fifteen guys had their minds blown," he said. Since his own father was present, he'd been more than just a neutral facilitator.

I listened, fascinated.

"But, Michael, I realize I am still in the Marlboro Man white male go-it-alone mode. I need someone else to lead this with me."

He was now staring at me with a meaningful look.

"Me?" I asked.

I was touched and suddenly my heart raced. I recognized this was a dream I couldn't pass up.

Outward Bound had been like a spiritual home for me,

where I found space to be myself and grow my facilitation skills. It was where I learned to trust and appreciate the experience-based learning model, and this was a shared background with Bill. Together, I knew we would address the white male side of diversity in a way that had never been done before. We would find a way for white men to connect to the white male part of ourselves—and each other—in a way that was positive and empowering.

Since that moment twenty years ago, we have held the White Men's Caucus more than 125 times in dozens of places. Each one is different yet very much the same. One unique setting was particularly unforgettable.

If you drive for a long time north of Houston, you will find yourself in the middle of nowhere. Finally, off the interstate, the road heads northeast through the swampy forest and arrives at Chain O' Lakes Resort—where a group of white men were about to have their essential beliefs challenged.

It was a late April afternoon, and the sun was waning as I sat on the porch of our cabin overlooking a pond. Bill and I were reviewing our plan for the next few days. The other men were in the process of checking in.

Bill gazed out through trees, admiring the lush surroundings. Every cabin had a pond next to it, and the forest was a thick, swampy place.

"Do you think there are alligators here?" Bill asked.

I looked out beyond the railing of the porch.

"Turn around," I said.

We saw a four-foot-long gator staring at us. I wondered whether humans or animals were in charge in this landscape.

"We better pass out flashlights," I said, "so we can see their eyes in the dark at night."

In more ways than one, we weren't in Kansas anymore! Later that afternoon, we visited our meeting room. It was windowless, and six rocking chairs were arranged in a circle with no tables. I felt a chill down my spine as I wondered what the guys would think about rocking together for four days. Four organizational leaders from three different organizations would arrive shortly. To say the least, this retreat center was off the beaten path. There was no looking back; whatever was going to happen here was about to happen.

That evening, all six of us dined at the Herb Farm restaurant onsite. A waitress told us about Snappy, the 300-pound snapping turtle that was more than 125 years old and hung out in the water under the deck. After dinner, we got a glimpse of him when he came up to eat. His head was the size of a grapefruit. One thing was for sure: this place had character. There were many other turtles and fish in the water, but they gave Snappy his space. He became our mascot for the week.

After dinner that night, six men sat themselves in rockers and we began. I was nervous as I knew our curriculum would be edgy for them. Bill and I opened by sharing how we came to this work and why it was limited to only white men.

In the midst of my talk, suddenly the lights went out. We found ourselves sitting in pitch darkness. I prayed it was a brief blackout.

Someone snickered.

"You planned this, right?"

We laughed nervously.

A soft light gradually entered the room as a waitress emerged holding a lighted candle in one hand and let us know it would be at least an hour before power was restored. It was the perfect metaphor for the process we were about to launch. We were entering the unknown, a place where all these men were in the dark.

In the candlelight, I said, "This might seem odd, but I want you all to grab another guy and go for a walk outside for fifteen minutes while we wait for the power. I want you to talk about what your hopes are for the week and what you might be worried about."

A small moan went up from the group.

"One more thing," I said. "I want you to share stories of what you told people before coming here. Did you tell them you were coming to a White Men's Caucus? What exactly did you say?"

After fifteen minutes, we all regrouped inside the restaurant, where there was some illumination from the fading daylight. We ended up huddling around some candles.

"Well this is probably your worst nightmare," Bill said. "You're probably wondering if we are going to sing 'Kumbaya.'"

Chuckles filled the room. I relaxed a few degrees.

"So tell me, what was your experience when you told others you were coming here?" I asked.

The men pondered briefly. Joe, a tall, fit analytic sort, who had expressed his skepticism from the second he arrived, shared that his wife rolled her eyes and said, "They are spending money on that?"

Al, a short, balding man who was heartfelt and sincere, owned up that his wife had said, "I'm glad you're going. You need this."

The other men laughed. Joe continued: "The people of color I work with were initially confused but then got excited, once they really got what it was about. I was afraid to tell them for fear they would think I was going to a Klan rally."

Frank was a real alpha-male executive. He had white hair and a square face, and he looked and acted like a general. He was now sitting upright in his chair. "I have to confess, on my flight here I turned the light off on my tray table while I was reading the Caucus material. I didn't want anyone to see the words: White Men as Full Diversity Partners.

A big laugh erupted before Frank continued his story.

"It didn't matter, though. The flight attendant saw what I was reading and asked, 'Are you part of an extremist group?'"

The room roared.

Bill held up his hands, indicating he had something to say.

"Which two words out of those six words do you think she noticed?" he asked.

"White Men!" someone blurted out.

I chuckled. Even after doing this work for twenty years I sometimes hesitated to have the words "White Men" front and center on my laptop or a paper document, for fear of being misunderstood.

Occasionally when Bill and I presented at companies,

we found the words "White Men" had been removed from the title of our session. When I asked why the name of the session had been changed, we were usually told, "We don't want to make anyone uncomfortable."

I reassured the group: "Your own discomfort is a good indication that you need to talk about it."

The men nodded and leaned forward in their seats. They seemed more curious. I sensed a bit of frustration, but the work continued. It would be another hour and a half before the power came on.

Lee, a quiet introvert with thick glasses, finally spoke.

"I thought I did something wrong to get sent here," he said.

"You're not alone," Bill said.

Bill began to explain: "At one of our conferences, there was a group of guys in the back row with their arms crossed and their eyes gazing down. They worked for a large equipment company. I went back and asked them why they were in the back row. Their answer was immediate: 'When this gets ugly, we want to be near the exit.'"

Bill continued: "Notice they didn't say *if* it got ugly, rather *when* it got ugly. There is an inevitable feeling that nothing good can come of this. White men believe they're about to be blamed for something. We feel like the human piñatas of diversity."

The men laughed in agreement.

Joe spoke up again. "The other thing that's confusing to me is what can I learn about diversity from a bunch of white men? Don't we need some people of color to learn from?"

I smiled. "That's what we've been taught, that we can only learn about diversity from women and people of color. That actually puts a big burden on them. Especially in an organization that is at least two-thirds white men."

Joe appeared skeptical.

I went on. "When you think about race, who do we usually focus on? Who is the topic of conversation?"

Al responded, "People of color."

"That's right," I said. "And when we focus on gender, who do we usually focus on?"

"Women," chimed in Joe and Frank.

"With sexual orientation, we focus on gay, lesbian, bisexual, and transgender people. So with the focus on people of color, women, and LGBT, we don't focus on or examine what it means to be white, male, or heterosexual," I said.

I scanned the room and saw surprise on all the men's faces.

"We don't generally know how being these things give us a unique experience in the world versus others. Addressing diversity by focusing on others makes us blind to what we most need to understand: our own experience."

I then explained that white men actually have more insights and personal freedom to gain from diversity than any other group.

"We're going to focus on those three dimensions—being white, male, and heterosexual—and on class. And we want you to bring in any dimensions of diversity that you want to explore, including age, religion, physical ability, and any others."

The men were staring at me blankly, speechless.

"We never think diversity is about us. We think it is about helping *those* people with their issues. We also look to them to be the teachers of diversity. How many chief diversity officers do you know who are heterosexual white men?"

In recent years, my partners and I knew of only two: Steve Bucherati at Coke and Frank McCloskey at Georgia Power, and they could see each other's offices from facing high-rises in Atlanta. They were the lone white wolves of diversity. Both are now retired. When McCloskey was named to his position, he took some flak from the black community in Atlanta, but his boss, the CEO, also knew he needed to send a message to the white men that diversity was about them too.

The guys seemed interested in all these revelations.

"So," I said, "off the top of your head, if you had to come up with one main goal here, what would it be?"

Al raises his hand. "I want to learn how gender and skin color influence my thinking."

Frank scoffed. "Al, you've already drunk the Kool-Aid!"

"Okay, Frank," I said. "What about you?"

Joe turned to him. "You gotta learn to listen, man!"

Frank scratched his head. "That's what my wife says."

The room went silent. Then Frank said, "Okay, I want to learn how to become a better listener."

Lee leaned into the group and adjusted his glasses.

"I want to know about my blind spots and how they have an impact on others. And I don't want to feel guilty about it."

Joe was staring at the floor.

"Joe?" I asked.

Usually about this time in the first evening someone expresses frustration. And, like clockwork, Joe piped up.

"Well, just what is the problem here? What are we trying to fix? If someone would tell me, I'd be much more willing to listen to this conversation," he said.

Al waved his hand.

"Yes, Al?" I said.

"Well, I know there's a problem. I have some women and some people of color in my center who are really open with me. They tell me they just don't like coming to work—because of feeling like outsiders."

Joe scowled. "I feel like I'm inclusive and I treat people fairly," he said. "There have been complaints filed against me, and others think I am biased. To tell you the truth, we spend way too much trying to address perceived inequalities. Is this a cancer? Because a few people have the cancer, we give everyone chemo?"

Frank seemed really annoyed. "Why do we have to walk on eggshells? When I travel for business, I notice women can tell sexist jokes. People of color can tell racist jokes. I can't. I'd get dragged to HR."

Lee quietly agreed. "It's isolating. If every interaction has to be documented, why do I even interact? It's too dangerous. So let's just have fewer interactions. I'll just stay by myself."

He seemed to be sulking.

At this point the tone in the room had heightened. Clearly a chord had been struck.

"I want to acknowledge all the frustration in the room,"

I said. "Whatever you are feeling is perfectly valid. We will have plenty of time to sort out our experiences. In the meantime, hang in there with whatever anger or fatigue you have. We don't often have a place we can talk about our experiences as white men. Our felt experiences can come pouring out when we create a space for this reflection."

I went back to Joe's original question about what we were trying to fix.

"We can't fix what we don't understand. A lot of our time here is going to be spent on understanding. You may not like it, but the more you understand, the more questions you will have."

I then made an announcement.

"I want you all to agree to give up your fix-it reflex," I said.

"Yeah, that will be hard. When I hear there's a problem, I try to fix it," Joe said. "It drives my wife crazy."

Amid a lot of grumbling, I began to lay out the new belief system I was proposing.

"Guys," I said, "here is your first Radical New Thought Habit."

And I presented . . .

MINDSET #1

It no longer works to see everything in life as a problem to solve. Life is a journey in which new questions and perspectives arise. The journey itself will lead to more profound learning.

THREE

Settling into the Living Room

BY THE NEXT MORNING, AS WE RECONVENED IN WHAT we came to call our living room, I noticed Joe was last to take his rocking chair. Bill and I settled in and prepared to start the day.

"Good morning. How did everyone sleep?" asked Bill. "Anyone encounter any alligators last night on the way to your cabin? Looks like everyone made it back with their limbs intact."

Chuckles filled the room.

After a quiet pause, Joe spoke up. "This whole focus on white men—aren't we just perpetuating stereotypes?"

I suspected his defenses were kicking in full force.

"You ask a simple yes or no question," I responded. "The answer can't be simplified with a yes or no. Yes, there is a danger of stereotyping any time you talk about a group. In my view, that is manageable in comparison to the larger danger of not examining our white maleness. By not examining that aspect of ourselves, we are blind to how that has shaped how we see and experience the world. Our experience is often profoundly different from that of white women and people of color. We don't seem to be aware of this."

Suddenly Frank angrily blurted out of nowhere, "But why does everything have to be about race and gender? Here we go again! Making us the evildoers of the world." He rolled his eyes and exhaled loudly.

"Tell me about it," Joe added. "May as well feed us to the alligators, or our buddy Snappy."

I noticed how Joe and Frank were feeding off of each other's skepticism. I wondered if any of the rest of the guys would follow them. Yet their bluntness was of value; it was now safer for anyone to say what was really on their mind.

Bill, a master at validating people, spoke up. "Frank, you're absolutely right, not everything has to do with race or gender. And, what happens when those issues do enter the picture, as they occasionally or sometimes frequently do? Are we willing and open to explore what that is about?"

Frank was right. It isn't always about race. In fact, one way to define diversity broadly is to ask: what differences make a difference? The answer is unique, depending on context. For some, it might be their age; for others, it's personality. But for many, race makes a difference. We all need to ask ourselves what differences make a difference, particularly with regard to the three questions we all struggle with in groups:

1. Am I in or out?

2. Do I have any power or control (voice or influence)?

3. Am I appreciated for my skills and resources?

Being white and male are not attributes usually examined or even considered by white men. But we shine a light on these unexamined aspects of diversity in order to comprehend their impact.

"I don't picture myself as being in a white male group," said Al, scratching his goatee.

"I think we are pretty universal about that," said Lee. "When I think of the words 'white men,' words like 'good ole boys' come up."

"Let's go there," I said. "What other words come up for you?"

I wrote the words "White Men" at the top of a blank flipchart page.

"Can't jump," scowled Frank with a little smirk growing on the corner of his mouth.

"Huh, how about 'can't dance'?" added Al.

"Founding fathers," said Lee, straightening his shirt front.

"How about Republicans, congress, executives?" added Al.

The guys in the room shouted out words as I scribbled them onto the chart. "Establishment, inventors, breadwinners, smoke-filled rooms, golf."

"White men . . ." I repeated, asking for more associations.

They began shouting out all the things popping into their minds.

"NASCAR"

"Good one."

"How about Aryan Nation," Joe suggested.

The group moaned.

"Well then, there's the KKK," Frank offered.

The groans continued.

Al jumped in with another slant. "I think we are also breadwinners, explorers, drivers." He looked around, wanting the group to see the positive side as well.

"Yes," said Lee who shifted his glasses on his nose. "But I'm also going to add what just came to me, which is 'insensitive and entitled'."

Bill made a shift.

"So let's hit the pause button," he said. "What do you notice about your reaction to what gets attached to those two little words?"

"I don't connect with most of that. Maybe some of it," Joe said.

"Much of it's pretty negative," chimed in Frank.

"Yes," I admitted. "All these associations for the words 'White Men' may make you even less inclined to want to see yourself as part of this group. There is a wide range of connotations attached to our group."

Bill added, "And I suspect this list won't make you proud to say you're a white man."

I smiled, knowing Bill's last name is Proudman.

Bill continued, "Now what happens when we add the word 'diversity' to those two words? Let's brainstorm for a moment. What assumptions do we and others make about white men related to diversity?"

Frank jumped in, "The assumption that's made is that we are the problem. It's like people think if we changed, somehow all the problems related to diversity would just go away."

"Not only that," Joe added, "people assume we don't care

about diversity. And we only support diversity because we have to."

"Yes," I added, "not only do people assume we don't care, diversity is one area where we as white men have negative credibility, and as individuals we must often prove we have some competence. Ironically, we're stereotyped too."

Lee, who had been listening intently, leaned forward. "I do feel like I have to prove I'm sensitive to diversity. The proverbial alligators are out there ready to bite my head off if I make a mistake."

Bill spoke, as he rocked back and forth steadily in his chair, "The environment of political correctness and zero-tolerance policies often make us withdraw. We think we're not going to stick our toes into this conversation because nothing good can come of it. Like you said yesterday, Lee, you just feel like keeping to yourself and not engaging."

"Yep," agreed Lee.

Bill continued. "No learning can come from disengagement."

Lee piped up, "My strategy is to fake it till I make it."

The guys were starting to agree that this is a messy situation we are in and that Bill and I aren't there to blame them. I felt my shoulders drop after taking in a big breath.

What was going on in the group was very familiar to me. I identified with all of the men as I thought about my own journey. Like them, I did not want to associate myself with everything negative attributed to white men. I remembered when my strategy was to keep my mouth shut so I wouldn't look bad.

As I sat there, I pondered the work my company had been doing with Catalyst, a global nonprofit research organization headquartered in New York City that has been researching gender in corporations for more than fifty years. They had interviewed many of our white male clients who had gone through the caucus program and were now engaging other white men in their companies around diversity issues. We are apathetic because we don't see there is a problem. We're fearful about making mistakes. We're also fearful of loss of status from other men's disapproval. Finally we're fearful of being perceived as ignorant.

I could now see all three of these barriers in the living room. Joe and Frank were slumped in their chairs, their apathy evident. When I glanced at Al, who was sitting shyly with his head bowed, I sensed his biggest fear was disapproval. He was afraid of fully expressing himself. As for the third barrier of ignorance, it was clear that the whole group was dreadfully afraid of being perceived as clueless white men. I knew the best way to get beyond these fears was not to censor them but to encourage their expression. Robert Frost once said, "The best way out is through." This is what was happening in the living room, and I was learning to trust the process.

Frank angrily piped in. "Look, I think we're beating a horse to death here. I think we are wasting our time."

He glared at Bill and me.

A hush fell over the room. No one wanted to challenge the alpha male. The next step would be crucial. It required simultaneously challenging and supporting Frank from a place of compassion. Tension choked the air.

Breaking the wall of silence, I spoke. "I hear your frustration. Seems like you feel stuck in a no-win situation."

I saw Frank's eyes open wider, and his face softened slightly.

At that point, I took a big risk.

"I hear your CEO is in the midst of a predicament. She thinks you're deaf to your customers," I said.

Frank sat still, listening, then glanced around the room. It was as if his armor had been removed.

"Yeah, she traveled around the country to find out what customers really thought. To put it bluntly, a significant percentage of our customers think we are arrogant, don't listen, and we try to sell them extravagant solutions that are more than they can afford," Frank said as he leaned back in his chair.

"Wow," Lee chuckled. "That's gotta hurt."

Frank had inadvertently foreshadowed our next mindset shift: *to gain a complete picture of the world, it is necessary to invite multiple perspectives.*

Frank was looking at me, puzzled.

"Our CEO obviously thinks that we don't get our customers' viewpoint," he said. "But I don't necessarily agree with her."

"That's interesting, Frank," I said. "You also don't agree with people of color when they raise issues they're experiencing."

Suddenly, Lee leaned forward and spoke up. "I kind of feel that way in here, Frank. That any perspective different from yours is not valid. What you have to say is insightful.

But hey, you know, the rest of us have some valid points too."

Frank was stunned. Al let out a little gasp and rocked back in his chair, wide-eyed, stroking his goatee. I wondered if he was moved by Lee's courage.

I smiled at Lee, knowing my own feedback to Frank had probably made it safer for Lee to speak his truth. By taking a risk, Lee had just created a safer living room for more honest dialogue. The barriers, such as fear of losing rank, were diminishing, and in fact, sincerity became a new way to gain status in the group. By letting barriers and concerns be expressed, they became opportunities to deepen our partnerships with each other.

Frank, to his credit, did not defend himself. He simply nodded to Lee. His face showed slight pain. It seemed to me that maybe the feedback was familiar to him.

I leaned slightly forward. "Well, Frank, holding your default mindset would make it harder for you to see a contrary perspective. Your CEO is focused on getting a more complete perspective from your customers. Not getting your customers' perspective eventually costs you business."

I gazed at Bill across from me. He said, "Frank, I really honor you for staying in the room and hearing these challenges. And Michael is right. Not getting the perspective of women and people of color in your organization also costs you in lower morale, less retention, and compromised partnerships across your team."

I'd seen similar shake-ups before. It's not that your view

of the world is *wrong*, I thought. It's more likely it's *incomplete*. I'd say that's true for all of us.

We usually accept our own realities as valid but question others when theirs are different from ours. When we let go of "right or wrong" and focus instead on being curious about what we don't see, big revelations occur. Our old habit of defending our limited worldview blocks our learning. The following radical thought habit is an alternative.

MINDSET #2

Incorporate multiple perspectives, even if they are contradictory. They give you a more intricate view of the world. Seeing the world from only one perspective gives an incomplete view.

FOUR

The Four Paradoxes

THE CHALLENGE OF SEEKING MULTIPLE PERSPECTIVES brings to mind the story "The Blind Men and the Elephant." Several men were engaged in an argument about God and different religions, and they could not come to an agreement. So they went to ask Buddha what exactly God looks like. The Buddha asked his disciples to get an elephant and four blind men. He then brought the four blind men to the elephant and told them to explore the appearance of the elephant.

The first blind man touched one of the animal's legs and said it looked like a pillar. The second blind man touched the elephant's abdomen and said it was like a wall. The third blind man touched the elephant's ear and said that it was a piece of cloth. The fourth blind man held the tail and described the elephant as a piece of rope. They all argued about the appearance of an elephant. The Buddha then asked, "Each man has touched the elephant but each gives a different description of it. Which answer is right?" In the group, the men were beginning to see that each had a piece of the truth, but none had the whole picture.

This story illuminates the nature of paradox. Many things can be simultaneously true and yet hidden depending on the position of the viewer.

Over the years, working with dozens of corporations, Bill and I came to discover there are four paradoxes in diversity partnerships.

Individual/Group is the first paradox. This is the conundrum of being a unique person with individual views but also part of a community, society, or group. For our men at the Caucus, one of these groups is white male. Being part of that group does not mean they must give up their individuality or uniqueness. As white men, we resonate more with being individuals and don't want to associate ourselves with being part of the white men group. Rugged individualism is what we were brought up on.

The second paradox is Sameness/Difference. It is the challenge of recognizing commonality—or shared qualities, attributes, and beliefs among different groups—and at the same time acknowledging the unique differences. Many managers tend to focus on just one side—sameness, for example—while neglecting legitimate differences for fear of being discriminatory. They think that treating everyone the same is a way to be fair. What most white men don't know is their definition of treating everyone the same is based on the white male norms. It becomes forced assimilation.

The third paradox is Support/Challenge. The most powerful learning happens in relationships where both of these forces are at work. The most powerful teachers in one's life challenge and support you at the same time.

The fourth paradox is Not My Fault/I'm Responsible. Often white men feel they are being asked to carry the personal burden of historic mistreatment of other groups. It is not their fault, and they are vital participants in the dialogue needed to create more equitable systems for everyone, including white men.

And sitting in this group of white men, I geared up for the next step. I knew these paradoxes could be tricky to introduce. Shifting the group forward, I proposed, "There is no better tool to explore multiple perspectives than the skill of balancing key paradoxes."

"Just what is a paradox, actually?" asked Joe.

"Two things that seem incompatible but are actually both true," I answered.

To illustrate this, I recounted "The Blind Men and the Elephant."

"In this story there is an argument over who is right. They don't see the paradox that each of them has a piece of the truth.

"Our white male culture, in my experience, emphasizes either/or thinking. A good example of this is 'You're either with us or against us.' Along the same lines, I've had white men ask me, 'Am I aggressive and competitive because of genetics or because I learned it in my culture?' That question assumes the cause is *either* genetics *or* culture. Such limited thinking and language precludes the more complex possibility that it's a combination of *both* genetics *and* culture. This approach prevents us from considering that each perspective sees a different piece of the picture and is how we miss the complexity and nuances of diversity. In every White Men's Caucus, guys ask me these either/or questions from a heartfelt place without even recognizing the inherent blind spot the question sets up. See if you can recognize it the next time it happens here."

"Is that a challenge or a learning point?" asked Joe.

"There's one. That didn't take long," said Al, as he scratched his goatee.

I rolled my eyes while laughing and continued. "The Leadership Skill of Balancing Key Paradoxes is about seeing the *both/and* rather than the *either/or*, that two options that seem incompatible can both be true. There are four paradoxes for us as white men to explore to get a more complete picture of diversity. Seeing them as paradoxes forces us to validate both as part of the complete picture."

I stood and uncovered another flipchart.

"I'm glad there are only four," chuckled Al.

"It's plenty to keep us busy for a while," I replied. "We've been struggling with these already, actually. The skill of balancing key paradoxes is a way to actualize the new thought habit of *incorporating multiple perspectives, even if they are contradictory.* Paradoxes are by definition contradictory."

"Tell me about it," blurts out Frank. "I didn't know that until yesterday."

Al piped in, "Yeah, I never thought about it before."

"I started on the first paradox. Our individuality is a given. There is no one else like you on the planet." I added, "But if you see everything through an individual lens, you may feel personally accused or attacked when someone is talking about our group rather than you. A police officer in a previous caucus said he used that information his first day on the job. He was in a situation that usually ends in a fight or an arrest, and he was able to avoid both. He was confronted by an angry person of color in public. He realized that the person was not talking to him as an individual. They had never met before. He was simply frustrated with all the white male officers he had dealt with before. The cop used the paradox to be able to listen differently with a different outcome. He didn't take the comments personally as about him."

"I've had that happen to me," said Joe. "When I was a police officer, I dealt with angry people every day who accused me of things. I never thought to connect their frustration to their experience with our group. I still remember that happening to me with a guy in the street one day, and I thought he was just a bit crazy and prejudiced against cops. It sure made me angry when he accused me of ruining his life. I see it even more often now that I am Police Chief."

Joe was the first to disclose his profession in the living room. Bill leaned toward him and said, "You're actually touching on the fourth paradox, which we call Not My Fault/I'm Responsible. We become preoccupied with defending our innocence and proving that we are good guys. It's especially easy to get defensive if we take their comments to be all about us personally. Meanwhile, because we are caught in a not-my-fault loop, being defensive and advocating our innocence, we are not at that time operating out of inquiry to better understand their world. Yet it is our *responsibility* to understand others' perspectives if we are going to partner with them. No learning happens when we are caught in the not-my-fault defensive loop."

"You're right," Joe replied. "There was no way I was going to ask him about his life experiences when I felt so blamed for all his problems."

"So what happened?" asked Lee, leaning forward in his rocking chair.

"Fortunately my partner started asking him questions, and that changed the conversation," replied Joe as he looked at the floor.

Al, who was listening intently, leaned into the conversation. "Joe, I am glad you are here and bringing your past experience as a police officer. I am excited to learn from you, and I want you to know I've been there—defensive and pissed."

Appreciating the empathy present, I added, "Notice which of these paradoxes are hardest to manage for you and lean into that one to gain a more complete picture and create more choice in how you respond to these situations. Sometimes a conversation is stuck because people are at opposite sides of a paradox unwilling to acknowledge the other. Either party can acknowledge the truth in the other's perspective."

The room was quiet, but I noticed the silence was no longer awkward; rather, it felt like a welcome moment for reflection.

Bill finally spoke, "How many of you have ever said this: I don't see color or gender. I just treat everyone the same?"

Most of the guys' hands went up, including my own.

"I still say that," noted Frank. "I told someone on my team that a few days ago." He glanced at Bill smiling. "Is that good or bad?"

"Busted. There's another one of those banned either/or questions," laughed Al.

"Al's onto it, man," I declared.

Bill continued, "This has to do with the Sameness/Difference paradox. We as white men often focus on treating everyone the same as a way to be fair and equal. So we attempt to be color-blind and gender-blind. Our intent is equality. But our impact on others is that they often feel like they have to be like us. Our standard of sameness is ourselves, using a culture we don't realize we have. But others fit into it, so they are well aware of our culture. What others hear is more like 'If you fit into my box and keep me comfortable, then I'll treat you the same.'"

"I don't buy this stuff about us having a culture," said Joe.

Lee retorts, "Yeah, you go around the world trying to fix everything, but you don't have a culture. Well, I don't think that fix-it habit is just your personality, Joe."

"We'll have plenty of time to wade into the cultural waters we swim in," I answered. "Right now I want you to consider the notion that a fuller picture of diversity comes from exploring ways we are the same *and* ways we are different. If you are in a business meeting, for example, notice our common humanity, common hopes and fears, and notice the differences in who gets heard. Be color-blind and color-conscious at the same time. If you default to seeing only sameness, then explore noticing difference. Most of us white men focus on individuals (vs. group) and sameness (vs. difference). By focusing on what we already know, we miss the stuff that's more frustrating to white women and people of color. Remember, too, the new mindset—incorporate multiple perspectives, even if they are contradictory. The paradoxes give us a map to explore multiple perspectives."

"What about the third paradox?" asked Frank.

Bill responded, "Yes, the paradox of *support* and *challenge*. Think about the more powerful mentors in your life. Chances are they supported you and challenged you to do better at the same time, sometimes in the same breath. This also creates the most learning in diversity partnerships. I am noticing that we are beginning to have that level of engagement here in our living room. We want you to support each other and challenge each other, including us, with differing perspectives."

FIVE

Seeing the Water
We Swim In

AFTER LUNCH WE SETTLED INTO OUR ROCKING CHAIRS.
Joe leaned forward and reiterated his skepticism that a white
male culture existed.

"I don't buy into this concept that there's one white male
culture. I think there is enormous variance across the country. The mannerisms, speech, all vary from New York, across
the South, in the Midwest, or out on the West Coast."

Bill responded, "You're right about the variances. Here
is one of those places to apply that second paradox. You
can look for and find *both* sameness *and* differences. I've
never said there aren't differences. There are *both* differences
and there are common threads. For example, this trait of
approaching most things as problems to fix is pretty well
shared across white men."

"I think most of us are proud of that," piped in Lee as he
wiped a speck off his glasses. "Though some of our wives get
tired of us seeing them as problems to fix." He glanced over
at Frank and Joe.

Frank raised his eyebrows in response. "Is what we are
talking about really just *business* culture? I've worked in

the military for many years. Seems to me, it's also military culture."

"Who founded the military and most businesses in our country?" I asked.

"Us," answered Al, as he scratched his balding head and glanced at the white men around the room.

I continued. "If we created most of the institutions we dwell in today, they are going to reflect our culture. But we don't see this cultural water we swim in because we never have to leave it. So we equate it with just being a good human. Others assimilate into it, so it looks to us like it's everyone's culture."

Frank interrupted, "What's wrong with our culture? Why is it suddenly so bad?" His face showed his disgust with me.

"Did you hear me say it was bad?" I replied, feeling slightly irritated while staring back at Frank.

"Look, this culture is why were successful," argued Frank definitively. "No one is going to tell me throwing it away is going to somehow make us better!" He sat back in his rocking chair and folded his arms.

I responded in a way that nobody expected. "I'm noticing my palms sweating, my heart racing, and I'm feeling defensive." The room grew quiet as I shared a revealing statement about myself that couldn't be argued. All attention in the room was focused on me. After a few seconds of everyone rocking in silence I continued, "I actually love my white male culture. I love that rugged tenacity and can-do attitude. For the most part, it has served me well, and I actually wouldn't be here otherwise."

I looked at Frank. "You're right, Frank, it has been a major contribution to the success of our society. Like any culture, it has upsides and downsides. I would not describe it as bad or something that needs to be thrown away."

"Then what exactly are you saying?" asked Frank suspiciously with his arms still folded.

I leaned forward into the circle with my pulse still beating strong. "First of all, I am saying that we do have common cultural characteristics, and they are mostly invisible to us. We seem to believe that we don't have a culture but that everyone else has a culture. Can you imagine telling the majority group in Japan or Germany that they don't have a culture? Part of our culture is our strong fixation on individuality. We cherish our ability to stand on our own two feet and make decisions freely. So the notion of being part of a cultural group goes against the very grain of our culture."

Frank squinted his eyes, still thinking. His arms came uncrossed and shifted down to his rocking chair arms.

"Second, I believe that our culture has great strengths. Third, when we overuse those strengths they can become weaknesses, which is why I am proposing the following radical thought habit."

MINDSET #3

Your strengths overused become weaknesses. Notice when your strengths don't serve you. Create the space to grow underutilized skills and attributes even if you feel tentative at first.

I could see many of the guys in the circle were taken back. I explained, "The research shows that most executives derail by overusing their strengths. In the book *Fear Your Strengths*, Robert Kaplan and Robert Kaiser propose that when leaders are doing too little of one behavior, there is an 80 to 90 percent chance they are doing too much of another corresponding behavior. Yet the focus is rarely on doing too much. The authors said that even the tools used to assess managers are not equipped to pick up on strengths overplayed. In fact, their database assessment results for 7000 executives show that only 10 percent of executives qualify as versatile." I added, "Other research from the Center for Creative Leadership shows that most executives derail by overusing their strengths."

Al leaned back in his chair and cleared his throat. "That rings true to me. I do have a colleague who was extremely detail oriented, and when he was promoted, he derailed because he was a micromanager."

I continued, "When something doesn't work, our first reaction is often to try doing the same thing harder. But the old adage is if you always do what you've always done, you always get what you've always gotten. We can overuse our strengths at a personal level. We can also overuse our culturally shaped strengths and habits."

I paused and scanned the room. "Any of you ever hear from your spouse or significant other 'I don't want you to fix this, I just want you to listen'?" I asked.

I noticed Frank, Joe, and Al all raise their hands.

Al spoke, "Maybe that's why my wife said I needed to come here."

"Both individual and cultural habits get in our way if we overuse them," I said. "As a result, our effectiveness in the world is compromised. It's clear that when we act on these overused strengths, we sometimes make things worse."

Bill leaped into the conversation. "So let's try an experiment. I invite each of you to share a strength you have and how, when overused, it can become a weakness. I'll go first. You probably have noticed that I talk quite a bit. I know my sharing can really serve men who are wandering into this complex terrain of diversity, and I share a lot of stories and experiences that stir reflection. I also know there are guys who can tune me out after a while. For them it can be too many words. And, Michael, I know sometimes you feel crowded out of the collective airtime in our co-facilitation." He paused, looking at me.

I nodded. "Yes. I do sometimes feel challenged to fit in my voice with yours."

I took note of the men while continuing. "The introvert/extrovert dimension is a dimension of diversity that Bill and I check in regularly about when we partner together." I noticed Lee regarding me with big eyes, nodding yes. The men sat quietly, surprised by our transparency. I was about to speak when another extrovert jumped in.

Frank opened his square jaw and shared his strength: "Confidence is a strength of mine. I am always self-assured, and that is why I am quick to assess a situation and take charge. My team still likes to call me The General, even though I'm retired from the military. I've done this my whole life. The truth is my siblings even called me General Frankie growing up."

Laughter erupted in the room.

"I'm not surprised," stated Joe. Joe was not laughing.

Frank paused, his eyes cast down at the floor. His demeanor shifted and he appeared lost.

"What else Frank?" I invited him to continue.

"I do turn people off. They see me as arrogant."

Lee nodded while watching Frank. He seemed relieved to see Frank own this.

"Right now I have a problem with my son," continued Frank. "Perhaps he's intimidated by me. He doesn't want to have anything to do with me, and I don't know how to change that." Frank's face flashed pain for a moment.

Joe leaned in. "Your overconfidence pushes him away?"

"Apparently," answered Frank as he stared back at Joe.

"That's tragic," chimed in Al, who had been listening intently.

Bill reached over and touched Frank on the shoulder. "Great example, Frank, of an asset that can also become a liability. I hope we can help you find new ways to connect with your son."

Frank nodded, still looking pained and perhaps embarrassed.

Al spoke next as he stretched his neck on his stocky frame. "I feel a lot and live in my heart. I notice others and seem to tune into what they are feeling, too. Others say I can bring the heart out in a room. I like this ability, but sometimes I get too caught up in what others feel. It starts mattering too much, and I end up spending my time making others happy. Along the way I lose track of my own perspective. I am like a chameleon adapting myself to those around me. I can forget who I am or what I want."

I was struck by the contrasting examples.

"Al, perhaps you could use some of Frank's confidence in exchange for some of your sensitivity," I said jokingly. Frank and Al stared at each other awkwardly with a shared sense of appreciation. I'm guessing they never thought of each other as role models before. Perhaps only as anti-role models.

Joe was staring curiously at Al at this point. He then offered, "I'm a clear, quick thinker and a fast problem solver. People come to me constantly to help them figure stuff out. So much so that sometimes they don't try to solve things themselves. They assume my solutions are better than theirs."

"Well are they?" quipped Al.

"Yes. I can see through a poor solution quickly. I feel it is my job to point it out," Joe said. "But it doesn't build confidence or get people to work independently. I am doing what I'm good at even if it means I'm not getting what I need from others in the long run."

"Lee?" asked Bill.

Lee was staring into the middle of the room in deep thought. He sat back, adjusted his glasses, and looked around at the men in the living room. "I think my best strength is that I am deeply reflective and I don't rush to conclusions. I seem to contemplate issues and questions and ruminate before making a decision. People who know me seek out my opinion. But my careful evaluations sometimes mean I don't share them quickly enough. I am not quick in putting my ideas out there. I resonate with Michael's challenge in being an introvert. The downside of my strength is that my slower, deeper reflection gets overlooked in our fast-paced organization."

"I do appreciate your wisdom, Lee," said Al. "And you are right, I've had to learn to seek it out. I wish you would push it out to us more without us asking. You're like a silent sage."

As he heard this, Lee straightened up in his chair, sitting taller, and pulled his shirt down to smooth out the wrinkles. "It's tough to inject ideas when I almost have to interrupt to get into the conversation. I've appreciated the slower pace of our conversations here."

I opened my mouth to talk as I heard Bill's voice.

"Thanks guys for that experiment," he said.

"You're welcome," said Frank. "But I still don't get what this has to do with a so-called white male culture." He seemed confused.

"Joe shared his analytic nature, Frank talked about his confidence, I talked about my extroversion, Al focused on his heart-centered approach, and Lee explored the downside of his deep thoughtfulness. I'm trying to get you all to see how overusing strengths operates at a personal level. Not only do we all overuse our strengths at a cultural level, there's a collective overusing of strengths. The things we are taught to emphasize in our white male culture—like confidence and being analytical—are especially vulnerable to being overused."

Bill then stood and revealed a flipchart page listing our view of some of the strongest tenets of white male culture in the United States. He shared them with the group.

CORE THREADS OF THE FABRIC OF WHITE MALE
CULTURE IN THE UNITED STATES

▸ Rugged Individualism

▸ Low Tolerance of Uncertainty

▸ Action over Reflection

▸ Rationality over Emotion

▸ Time Is Linear & Future Focused

▸ Status & Rank over Connection

Bill continued, "We're going to reference this list over the next few days. We're not asking you to agree with the items on this list but to just consider them."

Lee raised his hand.

"You go, Lee!" Al cheered.

Grinning, Lee shared, "I certainly relate to the emphasis on action over reflection. As an introvert and a deep thinker, I believe there is very little time for reflection built into most businesses."

Al added, "The rationality over emotion describes my experience many times when I bring a heart focus into work."

I observed, "Notice that the guys who bring the skills less emphasized in the culture can more quickly identify how the culture works against them. You might imagine the same experience for women and people of color."

The men sat pondering this new insight.

"You name these as cultural traits of white men in the United States?" started Frank. "Don't other business leaders around the world also hold some of these characteristics?"

"Yes," I answered. "Over the years we've had guys in the White Men's Caucus from Australia, New Zealand, South Africa, U.K., Germany, Netherlands, and Canada, to name a few. Most of those men related to these traits. They also articulate variances from some of them."

Bill jumped in. "Lately I've led quite a few sessions across Europe and Asia. There we are more likely to call it Dominant Business Culture. But it's the same process— helping the dominant group, in most cases, white men, understand they have a culture. Like fish, most of us are not aware of the water in which we are swimming. I am about to go lead sessions in India and China for leaders of U.S.-based multinational corporations. It's even more critical in today's global world that we as members of the dominant group understand our water. Not only do we swim in it, we often unconsciously expect others to conform to a culture that clashes with their own."

I noticed in those last few moments of our afternoon that several of the living room chairs were now rocking in sync.

SIX

Leaning into Complexity

MIDWAY THROUGH TUESDAY AFTERNOON WE PAUSED for a break, and the men were anxious for some outside air. The midday sun was gleaming off the pond just beyond the deck.

I stood by the railing and gazed down.

"Can you see him?" asked Joe.

Joe leaned over and joined me. There was Snappy with his long nose sticking out of the water. Frank strutted over, three-star General style, and likewise gazed downward. Behind him were Al and Lee.

Al had a piece of cornbread from the snack bar in his hand.

"Feed him," Frank ordered.

Al began crumbling bits of the cornbread and tossing them down to Snappy, who regarded us with a bored expression.

The crumbs were accumulating on his head.

As I watched, amused, I thought, there's just so much you can do when attempting to feed knowledge to any particular audience. I looked at Snappy again. Suddenly he was consuming the bits of Southern cornbread, and the men began to laugh. I smiled. It was partway through day two, and I had hopes the group would soon be fully digesting what they were being offered.

Bill nudged me.

"You kick off this next piece," he said.

"Let's begin," I said, and ushered the men into the living room.

"Welcome back," I said. I took a minute to reread aloud the men's goals:

► I want to learn how gender and skin color influence my thinking.

► I want to know about my blind spots and how they have an impact on others.

► I want to learn how to become a better listener.

"These are some of the things you all mentioned as your desires as we sat in the dark the first evening," I said.

Across the room I noticed Joe rocking fast in his chair. "What's on your mind?" I asked.

"I'm starting to figure this out," Joe blurted. "But it seems to me these issues are a whole lot more complex and emotional than I ever dreamed. I sure wish it could be simpler."

"What are you starting to figure out?" asked Lee.

Joe replied, "The whole issue of diversity is hugely inefficient. There are misunderstandings that waste time and money. Why isn't this easier to solve?"

"We are talking about humans here, Joe, not widgets," said Al.

Joe shook his head. "Look," he said, "I've got an African American male employee who turns every conversation into a race issue. He just always seems angry. He's blown up at me, reported me to HR, and I've been investigated."

The other men sat up in their chairs. He'd just confessed something important.

"So what happened with that?" asked Al.

"It's still pending," answered Joe nervously.

"How's his performance?" asked Frank.

"He's highly skilled and gets stuff done," Joe said. "I just don't understand why he has to be so emotional."

Bill was leaning on the edge of his chair waiting for an opening. He now jumped in.

"Do you know much about what his world is like?" Bill asked.

"Well, no. I know he is unhappy and doesn't have too many friends at work."

Bill pushed on. "So you wish he could tell you his concerns rationally, right?"

Joe nodded.

"You're assuming his style of communication is the same as yours," Bill said.

This is an important issue explored by linguist and anthropologist Thomas Kochman in his book *Black and White Styles in Conflict*. In his research of urban black culture in Chicago, he found *truth* is signified by the presence of emotion. In contrast, in Anglo culture, truth is signified by the absence of emotion.

That doesn't mean that every black man or woman is ultimately emotional, or that every Anglo person is exclusively rational. It's more complex than that. Individuals are unique regardless of the truths of the group.

Bill continued, "Emotion is a problem for you, Joe, not for him. I can imagine your colleague has received many messages to tone it down as he assimilates into your workplace, and that is yet another source of frustration for him."

"So what are you suggesting, Bill?" asked Joe, his face reddening with frustration. "That any emotion goes?"

"I'm suggesting there may be more room you can create for him to be himself."

"This is the place for another thought habit shift," I said. "We need to stop forcing other humans to conform to what is comfortable to us. Always having to be calm, rational, and neat dampens free expression and vivacity."

> MINDSET #4
>
> Learn to accept ambiguity, emotion, and discomfort.

Joe reacted. "Do you realize you're asking me to step onto another planet? Why would I do that? I don't even know what ambiguity is. I'm paid to keep it at bay. I was once in a job interview and the woman asked me how I deal with ambiguity. I remember thinking, 'What the hell is ambiguity?'"

The other men laughed, but they realized Joe was serious.

"Wow," chimed Lee. "You really don't know what ambiguity means?"

"Nope," replied Joe, proudly. "Things are pretty clear cut and rational in my mind. Emotion and uncertainty just get in the way. The public doesn't pay me to be vague and emotional."

Frank, who had been unusually quiet, leaned forward. "Joe, similar to you, my customers don't want much uncertainty in their product. I think this allowing of emotion and ambiguity can go too far."

"But who decides what is too far?" asked Bill. "Who sets the norm for what is acceptable?"

"We do," answered Lee.

Al had been listening intently as he pinched his goatee. "This preference for rationality impacts me too. I find myself continually censoring my emotion so as not to be accused of being too soft or too irrational. I'm tired of it. I just want to be myself."

"You and many others," Bill said. "Many men and women have to suppress their emotion in our white male culture."

To illustrate his point, Bill shared a conversation he'd had with an African American man who had been in one of our corporate mixed race and gender Allies Labs. The man had a gentle manner. Bill asked him why he was always smiling. Was he always as sweet as a teddy bear? The man answered yes. Then he paused and said, "Actually, no."

He proceeded to tell Bill how, when he'd entered corporate America twenty years earlier, he'd quickly discovered that his natural demeanor scared people and he had to tone it down. He'd learned to stand in elevators with a smile on his face. "Now my son doesn't even know who I am," he said, teary-eyed, "because I am not just like that at work, I am like that all the time."

The men sat stunned at Bill's story.

Bill turned to Joe. "How might we learn to accept people being themselves?"

Joe glanced around the room, mystified. "I don't think there is room for emotion in the workplace. Things can just get out of hand. Where would it stop? Next thing you know there will be fistfights."

That was when I told the group about Kochman's research on culturally influenced perceptions. When voices are raised, Anglos perceive an intent of violence and judge the interaction as a fight. However, for urban blacks in Chicago, a fight isn't a fight until someone makes a move. There is plenty of room for spirited dialogue without it being a fight. Emotion and reason are not seen as working against each other in that culture.

Joe stared at me blankly.

I reminded them that one of the traits of white male culture we'd listed was low tolerance for uncertainty and ambiguity. Though we think we can't be rational *and* emotional at the same time, recent brain research demonstrates that emotion often plays a key role in decision making. When individuals have injuries to areas of the brain associated with emotion, they have a hard time making decisions.

"Think about the most important decisions in your life—where you live and who you partner with or marry," I said. "There are actually lots of emotions involved in those decisions."

"That's true," said Joe. "But I've never felt like emotion goes with my rational analytic mind. I never realized that was my cultural bias. I thought it was a universal truth."

"Try this on for size," Bill began. "Studies show that African Americans follow the notion of *truth before peace*. That is, being direct is of higher value than keeping people comfortable. In contrast, white men live more by *peace before truth*. That is, don't rock the boat and don't ask, don't tell. We do like direct assertive communication but not at the expense of what *we* would describe as strong emotion or discomfort."

Joe was clearly agitated. "So now you want me to become a fighter?"

"Listen," Bill said, "let's go back to your black colleague, Joe. He may be taking a position of truth before peace, and may be signifying his truth by showing his emotion. If you judge his behavior from your own cultural beliefs, you will misinterpret his behavior and perhaps even label him as being combative or irrational."

"So what do you want me to do?" Joe asked.

"First be aware that you have assumptions," Bill replied. "Then I invite you to stretch your comfort zone around uncertainty using the Leadership Skill of Leveraging Ambiguity and Turbulence."

Bill was mentioning a critical skill that runs against the grain of white male culture. The Calvinist roots of white male culture predispose us to either/or thinking. We yearn for clarity and to see situations in black and white. We want a wallet card to tell us the ten things to do and not do around diversity. But it can't all be so simplified.

I leaned toward Joe. "Are you willing to acknowledge when you are confused and accept the discomfort of emotion and uncertainty rather than run away from it?"

Joe, who had been leaning back in his rocking chair, wiped a bead of sweat off his forehead with the back of his hand. "Maybe."

"Maybe?" I repeated. "You're usually pretty certain. But now suddenly you're uncertain about accepting uncertainty."

The men around the room laughed at the irony. Joe cracked a grin himself.

"Okay," he responded, continuing to laugh at himself.

I continued, "You aren't getting what you want from people at work because you can't stand the uncertainty of letting others attempt to solve problems in ways different from your solutions. Right?"

He nodded and let out a sigh. "That's killing me. I gotta find a way to let go of holding onto everyone's work."

Bill chimed in, "You're in the right place, Joe. There's plenty of ambiguity here to get used to."

Al looked at Joe with interest. "I like the idea of you sharing more emotion, Joe," he said. "I sometimes feel like you're the Tin Man—without a heart."

Joe sat back and a flash of pain passed across his face. I wondered if he had heard that before.

It reminded me of a time when I worked with a printing company where the old CEO had been a trailblazer in diversity. I was scheduled to make a presentation during a meeting of the new CEO, who was a white male, with his diversity council. I watched his interaction with the council as I waited my turn to present. I noticed that he answered every question from his head. When we took a break, I asked several members of the council, "Did you get what you needed in that last discussion?" "No," they replied. "We don't know if he really stands for diversity. Does he really believe in it? Is he passionate about diversity?" His rational approach didn't connect with those who wanted to feel his heart and passion.

"There are many white men like you, who aren't comfortable connecting their hearts with their heads. They're tin men, too," I said.

"Actually," started Joe, "I do show anger at work."

"Me too," added Frank.

"That is one emotion we do seem to have more permission to share," I replied. "I'll bet many of you can tell stories of old bosses who took it to an extreme, pounding the table and dressing people down in front of everyone."

Frank agreed, "Living through those guys was like a rite of passage. They make me seem like a teddy bear."

Lee, who hadn't spoken for a while, adjusted his glasses and said, "If you go into a rage these days you get sent to HR."

"It still happens but in a more toned-down way," added Bill. "And it's more accepted when us white men get angry than when women or people of color do the same."

"That's not true," Al protested. "I know a white woman who can intimidate everybody."

"She probably had to learn that behavior in order to survive and be viewed as competent," replied Bill. "There are some white women who are better white men than many of us."

"Yup," stated Al.

"But how many of us lead with vulnerability?" I asked. "How many lead with fear, sadness, or by simply saying 'I don't know'?"

"That doesn't get you far," shouted Frank.

"We've learned to show no chinks in the armor," Bill said. "Yet if we want to be trusted and build partnership, we have to step out of our comfort zone and become more comfortable being uncomfortable."

I looked around the room. Bill was leaning back in his chair with arms stretched over his head. Coffee cups and plates littered the floor, and Al and Frank had their shoes off. Joe was picking a piece of lint off of Lee's shirt.

I smiled. "It's okay to have raggedy conversations because as humans we are inherently emotional, and relating to others can be messy."

"I'll take real messiness any day over fake composure," laughed Al. "Including our own scruffiness in the last day and a half."

SEVEN

Feeling the Weight of Oppression

BY THE END OF DINNER, I SAT WONDERING IF SNAPPY had finished eating the cornbread crumbs we shared with him and wanted more. For their part, the men in the room were growing more eager for what Bill and I were sharing with them.

As they returned to their seats with cookies from the dessert table, I asked, "How many of you have had someone in a hotel lobby walk up to you and hand you their car keys?"

The men looked at each other dumbfounded. They had no idea what I was referring to.

"None of you?" I asked. "How about you, Bill?"

"Hasn't happened to me, either, but it's a regular occurrence for the African American minister who married my wife and me. He is constantly mistaken for the valet while standing in hotel lobbies. People just walk up to him and hand him their car keys. It's irritating. He says one of these days he is going to thank them and keep the car."

The men laughed in disbelief. "I would venture to guess that rarely happens to white folks," continued Bill.

We were about to take a deep dive into exploring race. But not in the traditional approach used by most people. When race is the topic, the focus is almost always on people of color. The discussion is about blacks, Latinos, Asians, and others. Rarely is the attention on whites. It's as if white isn't a race. We were about to explore a common blind spot for white men, turning race inside out and exploring whiteness. One experience of being white is not ever being mistaken for the valet.

"Many of you have kids right?" I asked. Most of the men nodded.

"How many of you have felt that for the safety of your child you *had* to have a conversation with them about race? For example, have you told your children what they might get called and not to take it personally, and what to do and what not to do if they were ever stopped by the police?"

No one raised their hand.

"I told my kids to respect everyone and don't take crap from anyone," said Frank.

"That's great," I said. "So you never had to educate your kids about racism for their own daily physical safety?"

"No. My talks were never about race—they were about respecting everyone as human beings," replied Frank.

"Exactly," I said. "We as white men tend to focus on everyone as individual human beings and treating them all with the same respect."

"Yep," said Frank, annoyed.

"Put your last statement into the context of the first two paradoxes we discussed yesterday. We focus on *individual* human beings versus noticing the impact of racial *groups*. We also notice the *sameness* while downplaying the *differences* between our experiences and those of other racial groups," I said.

"So let's venture to the other side of those paradoxes and get curious about ourselves as a group of white people and what's different in our day-to-day lives from those of people of color. For instance, we can choose whether to even discuss race with our kids. It's optional. We don't have to warn our kids about their race."

"That's true," piped Lee.

I continued, "Seeing those larger patterns is a function of using the Leadership Skill of Seeing and Thinking Systemically. It's about noticing the many differences that play out in groups in terms of who is included, heard, and appreciated for their skills. This adds layers of complexity beyond only seeing everyone as individuals. With race, it means being color conscious."

Bill remained seated as he explained, "Seeing systemically is about noticing the bigger patterns of how our lives are different from folks of color," he said. "I might teach my son to speak up for himself and to challenge authority. Meanwhile, parents of boys of color often teach their kids to do the opposite if ever stopped by the police. As one man of color said in one of our sessions, 'I keep my hands on the steering wheel until the officer is beside me. I then tell him that I am going to open the glove box to get my registration. I then do that. I explain each step to him before I act.' That's a different world than I live in as a white man."

"But I've been harassed by the police," chimed in Al. "I am not immune."

"You had a similar experience, and you assume it is the same," I noted. "But it rarely happens to us, while it is a regular occurrence for people of color."

As I rocked in my chair I remembered one of our learning labs focused on mixed race and gender groups held south of Tucson with a national insurance company. Four managers took a ride across the Mexican border during the late afternoon break. There were two white men in the front seat and two black women in the back seat. They pulled up to the border officer, and the white guys chatted away, engaged in conversation. They were having a great time chatting with the border officer and were in no hurry to end the conversation. The women in the back seat were having a different experience. Their palms were sweaty and they were anxious to get out of there. They surprised the white men, as they drove away, when they asked, "What was taking you so long to get out of there?" The white men had no idea how uncomfortable black women were as a result of their prior experience with the law officers.

It was a perfect example of how we can live in two parallel universes. We are blissfully unaware of the vastly different experiences we have in the very same situation.

I saw that Frank was going to blow a gasket. He was redder than I had ever seen him. It was quite a contrast with his white hair.

"Frank?" I said. The other guys halted when they saw his bloodshot face.

"Actually, I have had experiences where my race counted against me," he said loudly with a vein bulging in his neck. "I went to a good school, got the grades, and worked hard to succeed in my first several jobs. I was at the top of my game, having run several critical operations at one company. A new job came open that was a great step up and I interviewed for it. I thought I was a shoe-in, but I didn't get the job. My HR buddy told me later that they had to give it to a minority. I'm over it now, but it upset me."

His face was still red.

"I don't believe you, Frank," said Bill. "You don't look over it. You still appear to be pretty upset about it."

"No. I'm over it," Frank yelled.

The men laughed.

Frank's eyes darted around self-consciously and he got quiet. The whole room felt still.

Bill spoke next. "Why are you directing your anger at the minority who got the job rather than the white men who were deciding who got the job? Was it actually white men who made the decision?"

"Yes," answered Frank as he nodded slowly. "Actually three white men and one white woman."

"Frank, did you feel like they were giving *your* job to a minority?" I asked curiously.

"Absolutely," said Frank.

"Notice I didn't say *the* job. I said *your* job," I replied. "The sense that it was yours and taken away reflects a sense of entitlement that we as white men can hold without even realizing it."

Lee, who had been listening intently, adjusted his thick glasses and began to speak. "I want to point out a few advantages that I notice you had in this instance, Frank. First, you were able to get the schooling you needed, especially at a 'good' school, as you said. The other applicant may not have had those opportunities. Second, you also had the track record of the jobs you did before this occurred. Third, you could bounce to another job, as I know you did. And fourth, you had an HR buddy in your network. Coming from a lower class background, I know not all white men have those opportunities. So class can have a role, too, not just race. What did you do once you were rejected?"

Frank answered, "My wife had just gone back to work, and she told me it was okay to quit and look for another job."

"So," said Lee, "that's another advantage—having a working spouse that you can rely on for transitioning."

I noticed Al took a deep breath and was nervously tapping his foot. Finally, he said, "Frank, there's something I want to tell you. You and I were here early Monday and had lunch with Joan, our colleague who was here for another conference. You looked at me most of the time and only occasionally glanced at her. I'm fairly sure she was irritated by that. If you did that type of behavior during your job interview, that could be another reason you didn't get the job. Your HR buddy may not even know that."

Frank seemed surprised. "Wow. I didn't know I was doing that."

"You might want to talk to her when you get back," said Al.

In five minutes time, the myriad complexities of human interaction had come up; it wasn't simply about minorities having unfair advantages.

"We will give you some tools to address what's really going on," I said.

"One more thing, Frank," said Bill. "I assume that experience that remains so strong in your memory happened a while go?"

"Twenty years ago," replied Frank.

"Wow. So it was a rare experience," suggested Bill. "I want to ask you something. What if that was a regular occurrence?"

"That would be exhausting and discouraging," responded Frank.

It was one thing to have an intellectual understanding of continual discrimination and oppression, but quite another to experience it emotionally and feel its impact on one's body. Bill and I exchanged glances. I knew we were both thinking the same thing. Should we inject an edgy exercise we had used frequently in the early days of our White Men's Caucuses? We stopped using it some years ago after one man from a hydroelectric power plant later acknowledged that he'd cracked one of his ribs doing it. If we did it, we'd have to manage it safely.

"Frank, are you willing to try an experiment?" I asked.

To my surprise Frank rose out of his chair.

"Thanks for being courageous, Frank," I said. "Now go to the center of the circle and kneel down."

He did as I asked and glanced around in anticipation. "Here's your chance to get me back, guys," he said.

"I need three volunteers to come forward," I said.

"Awesome," said Lee, who smiled as he rose out of his chair and rubbed his hands together.

Joe and Al quickly jumped out of their chairs to join the experiment.

"That was a little too easy to get volunteers," said Frank laughingly.

Bill spoke up. "I just want to say that Frank or any of us can decide to stop the activity at any point."

"Pick a word to signal you want to stop," I said.

"Turtle," said Frank.

The men laughed. "Gonna try and draw strength from Snappy, are you?" cried Joe.

It was amazing how quickly the male bantering commenced at just the thought of getting physical.

"Before we start," I added, "I want to impress upon you that it is okay to use the safe word and stop the activity if you sense the possibility of anyone getting hurt."

"Frank, do you have any injuries we should be aware of?" I asked.

"Stay away from my right knee," Frank replied.

Bill placed a small couch pillow under Frank's knee.

I went to Joe, Al, and Lee, and whispered their instructions.

They all got on their knees surrounding Frank. They rested their hands on Frank's back while Frank was on all fours on the carpet.

"Ready?" I asked.

"Ready," Frank said as he began to take some deep breaths.

"I simply want you stand up, Frank," said Bill.

Frank made a move to spring up from the floor, but Joe moved down quickly like a wrestler folding his long body over Frank's back at a ninety-degree angle. His weight was now lying across Frank's back. Frank sank back down to the floor.

Suddenly Frank again sprang upward, taking Joe with him. Al, however, was right there and threw his thick body over the top of Joe. Lee was standing near Frank's head, bent over, focused on pressing his hands into Frank's shoulders and passing his weight and strength down through his arms. Frank remained pinned to the floor. Suddenly Frank dropped his right side down while lifting his left, trying to throw Joe and Al off. The men rode him like a bronco. Frank's strategy didn't work. He tried throwing them off from both sides. All four men were now breathing heavily.

Then Frank let out a scream and stirred like a wild man. Joe and Al moved with him like they were attached appendages, while Lee kept Frank's shoulders fixed. Frank remained powerless to stand and began to curse as he continued to try to wiggle free.

"Turtle," Frank said.

Instantly the struggle stopped. Lee let go of Frank's shoulders, and Al got off Joe. Finally Joe raised himself off Frank, who collapsed onto the floor and lay there resting. Joe and Al also lay on the floor, with Lee kneeling nearby.

For ten seconds the only sound was four men breathing heavily.

After a moment, I asked, "Frank, what did you notice as you did that exercise?"

"You guys are strong," Frank said. "I thought I stood a good chance, but eventually I couldn't budge."

"Did you feel trapped?" I asked.

"I absolutely felt trapped. I felt helpless. My chances were slim to none."

I leaned toward Frank. "If that was your daily experience—perhaps not at this physical intensity, but at some subtle level you felt drained every day, like you were pushing a boulder uphill—how might that impact your world?"

"I'd be exhausted and develop a bit of an attitude," said Frank.

"Like the black colleague Joe works with?" asked Bill.

"Yeah," said Frank, panting. "I'd be tired of the unyielding burdens."

The men looked at each other with a sense of camaraderie, having survived a challenge that bonded them.

EIGHT

Exploring
White Privilege

ONE ASPECT OF THE LEADERSHIP SKILL OF THINKING
and Seeing Race Systemically was illuminated by a white
woman named Peggy McIntosh, who teaches at Wellesley
College. She had been aware of the privileges her male
professor colleagues enjoyed and decided to explore what
privileges she might enjoy being white. It took her quite
a few months, but she eventually came up with a list and
called it her Invisible Knapsack of Privilege.

I've recognized it myself, in many situations. I also know
there are many times when I'm still blind to it. For example,
I'm never followed around or accused of stealing anything.
In contrast, one black vice president who was in a learning
lab recently shared that when he goes shopping and comes
in with another bag, he goes right to an employee at the
check-out area and hands over his bag to keep behind the
counter. He is tired of being followed while shopping and
accused of shoplifting.

Another vice president, a white woman with an adopted
black son, told how her son is constantly stopped by the

police while driving home in the suburbs. She finally got so tired of it, she had an affidavit signed to keep in the glove box that proves he is her son and has a right to drive her car in their neighborhood. In contrast, my teenage daughter recently got her license, but I know I will not need an affidavit to shield her. She will likely never be stopped and accused of stealing a car or of being in the wrong neighborhood.

That afternoon in the Caucus, we pushed further into exploring what it means to be white, issues that are at the heart of the Leadership Skill of Seeing and Thinking Systemically.

As I stood next to the flipchart, I proposed a working definition of privilege:

> Systemic advantage or privilege is the unspoken, unacknowledged (and often invisible) benefits that are available to people through no actions of their own, but appear to those who have them to be available to any person who wants them. Systemic advantage or privilege is often more apparent to those who don't experience it.

Frank, who was no longer breathing heavily, raised his eyebrow. "I get what burdens others can feel like discrimination. But I don't feel privileged. I talked earlier today about how I've worked hard to earn everything I have."

"Here again is a *both/and* situation," said Bill. "No one is saying you haven't worked incredibly hard. We all have, *and* we may have also had the wind at our back. Privilege is not so much what you have but what you don't have to routinely think about or negotiate. Having privilege doesn't somehow make you wrong, and it's not something you chose."

"Everyone has some privileges," I added. "Think about the privilege of all of us who are temporarily able-bodied. The several times I have woken to a fire alarm in a hotel, I have been able to walk out myself without waiting for someone to come help me."

"Me too," said Joe, who was glad to be back in his comfortable chair.

"I also generally enjoy a clean, well-kept hotel room," I added.

"What do you mean?" asked Joe.

"A Hispanic vice president in a learning lab stayed in a well-known national hotel chain. The room stunk really badly. In the morning he told the manager. The manager said, 'Oh, I'm sorry. That's where we put all the Indian people. They like it there.' He couldn't believe what he heard," I said. "That's never happened to me, as a white man."

Joe shook his head in disgust.

"Most of us don't know this is going on in the background for our colleagues of color," said Bill. "Being white means we are not navigating stuff others deal with, lots of big and small stuff that adds up cumulatively. Think of it as death by a thousand paper cuts. This doesn't mean we don't get our own occasional paper cuts or mistreatment as individuals."

The men sat in reflection as we asked them to brainstorm examples of white privilege in the journal pages of their workbook. After a while, I read the following examples.

TEN EXAMPLES OF WHITE PRIVILEGE

1. I can go into a hairdresser or barber shop and find someone who can cut my hair.

2. I can easily buy posters, picture books, greeting cards, dolls, and toys featuring people of my race.

3. I can take a job with an affirmative-action or equal-opportunity employer without having my co-workers on the job suspect that I got it because of my race.

4. I can choose public accommodations without fearing that people of my race will be unwelcome or will be mistreated.

5. I can choose blemish cover or bandages in "flesh" color and have them more or less match my skin.

6. I can be pretty sure I will never be asked "Do you speak English?" or be told "You speak English very well."

7. I can make mistakes, fail miserably on a project, or be fired from a job, without anyone attributing this to my race.

8. Other people of my race can fail in positions they are ill-suited for, and it does not impact how others view my qualifications for a similar position.

9. I am generally part of the race majority in most higher-level work meetings I attend.

10. I can easily find mentors of my racial background at all levels in my organization.

The men sat silent in contemplation.

"That's not stuff I have thought about," said Frank.

"Me neither," added Al.

"What other examples did you come up with?" I asked.

Joe spoke first. "People are not surprised about my level of income, profession, or level of intelligence. Others do not perceive me as a threat."

I noticed Lee nodding.

"Lee?" I asked.

"I can go wherever I want whenever I want, for the most part. I am not questioned whether I belong—in a neighborhood, at a private club, on the tee box before noon on weekends, shopping . . ."

"I can show up fully as myself—I don't have to assimilate into being someone else," said Frank.

"Actually I am aware of assimilating, as I said before, in masking my emotion," challenged Al.

"That's true Al," I answered. "We as white men all assimilate into the culture. And at the same time, because we've been raised in it, we also know the rules and adapt without thinking about it."

"What did you write, Al?" I asked.

"I can talk about my history without being told to 'get over it,'" answered Al.

The men sat there staring at him silently. Lee appeared to be deep in thought.

"There's more," Al added. "I likely have more access to more networks of influence in my organization. Other white men may be more willing to take risks in sponsoring or recommending me for promotions."

"I still don't like the word *privilege*," said Frank as he looked around at the other men.

I watched Frank, knowing this was a common reaction that I've observed from white men over the past twenty years.

Most of us have a deep belief in meritocracy. The word "merit" in Latin means "earn." It's a belief that if we go out and pull ourselves up by our bootstraps and work hard, we can make a place for ourselves. Many executives have done exactly that and feel their lives are examples of hard work that has paid off. They often climbed farther than their parents could. That further reinforces the notion inside them that, "If I can do it, so can you." The corollary is that if you haven't made it, you're just not trying hard enough. We remain blind to the systemic barriers others spend time and energy negotiating.

Over the years, I've come to believe that most white men want the playing field to be level and everyone to have a fair chance. We assume that it is level and attempt to create equality based on a notion of treating everyone the same. However, we don't realize the standard of treating everyone the "same" is based on a white male norm, and that others are assimilating into our world. Our intent is equality; however, our impact on others is assimilation.

Having privilege does not take away from the reality that we have worked hard. But it feels like that to us. And it can be disturbing to realize we've had advantages we didn't know we had, that the wind has been at our backs, because we have never had to turn around and face the wind against us, something others deal with on a daily basis. We live in a parallel universe, assuming the world is the same for those around us.

People of color have a hard time realizing that we actually don't see our white privilege. Some believe we are simply trying to hoard our power. This negative intent gets projected onto white men, which then becomes a barrier to partnering with people of color. I sometimes tell people of color they're giving us too much credit. We are not mean, just clueless. We don't see or get the extent of our privilege.

"Just continue to notice your reaction, Frank, and sit with it," said Bill. "It's important that you come to your own conclusion about it. Don't just take our word for it. You might even find a different word that fits better than privilege."

"I actually don't feel the same amount of privilege as many of you," stated Lee. "I grew up in a very poor family, and we didn't have much. We lived in a mobile home most of my childhood, and I was often left alone as a boy while my mom went to work."

"How many siblings did you share a room with, Lee?" asked Bill.

"My two brothers and I had the same room growing up. We had a bunk bed and a single bed," answered Lee. "My two sisters shared another room. I was the first in my family to go to college."

"You are bringing another dimension into this conversation on white privilege," I said. "While we all share privileges from white skin, economic privileges are unevenly distributed among us. Class is a separate issue from race, and the relationship between them is also complex."

I was glad Lee injected the issue of class. It was an unspoken differential among the white men in the room. White men from poor or working-class backgrounds often have a hard time recognizing their white privilege because they identify so much with their economic struggle. Both are important realities to comprehend. The men could learn from the class differences in the room and use them to gain insights personally and to create inclusive organizations.

"How is it to actually acknowledge your class background with these guys right now, Lee?" I asked.

"I feel like an outsider," Lee said.

"I have a question for you Lee," I said. "What if you had told me what your experience was around your class upbringing? Perhaps you told me that you had to work twice as hard, that people ignored you, and that people assumed you were not competent."

"Yes, I could have told you that," answered Lee.

I continued, "Then suppose I told you something like the following. 'Well, that's not been my experience. I think you just need to try harder.' How would you feel, Lee?"

Lee's shoulders dropped and he let out a sigh. "I would feel angry. You just invalidated and discounted my reality."

"Exactly," I replied. "People of color often feel that way when they are sharing their experiences with us. In our intent to understand—and fix—we cross-examine them and question their reality, which puts them in the position where they feel they have to prove it's real to us. They might even stop to wonder, why even bother? Thus, the Leadership Skill of Listening is one of the most important skills for us to practice. This is shifting away from the idea that listening is either a precursor to debate or a tool used before fixing something. We are encouraging the move toward listening *to understand*. Listening to understand doesn't mean we agree. It means we hold each other accountable for getting each other's worlds."

In every White Men's Caucus, I always ask the men to choose one leadership skill they most need to work on. Listening is by far the one chosen most often. The attributes of white male culture, such as action, doing, and fixing, can crowd out our capacity to listen with the intent to understand and validate. Most white male executives move so quickly through their day from one meeting to the next that they don't feel they have the luxury to listen. The default can become listening just enough to attempt to finish people's sentences and impose solutions. These same leaders will complain about the leaders above them not taking the time to listen, not realizing those below are saying the same thing about them. One must reframe one's beliefs to consider listening as an essential action rather than an extravagance.

If you have heard from people of color, "You just don't get it," you may not be applying a systemic perspective and may not be listening in a way that makes others feel heard and understood. One of the reasons is that our auto-pilot mode is geared toward advocacy more than toward inquiry. The majority of time is spent arguing our position rather than understanding others' perspectives. This thought habit shift goes hand in hand with mastering the Leadership Skill of Listening.

MINDSET #5

Inquire and seek the insights of others. Maximizing inquiry will expand learning and create new partnerships. Most of us spend an overwhelming majority of our time in advocacy, arguing our positions and proving that our views are right. There is another way.

I looked at Al as he pondered my question about being invalidated. The shift from advocacy to inquiry is a crucial move when dealing with conflict. The Harvard Negotiation Project conducted research on unresolved conflicts between people. In analyzing the audio transcripts, researchers found that more than 90 percent of the time people were advocating their positions to the other party. Less than 10 percent of the time was spent in inquiry, asking questions to understand the other. In order to create a learning conversation that can break through conflict, we must reverse that ratio and eventually maintain a balance between inquiry and advocacy.

Edgar Schein, author of many books on organizational culture and leadership, recently published a book called *Humble Inquiry.* He expressed that we emphasize *doing and telling* in our business cultures, which cuts off critical learning. This can lead to costly mistakes, be it in the operating room, airport control tower, or wherever. When we ask questions that we don't know the answer to, we are using humble inquiry.

"I get it," said Al. "Part of what it means to be white is we don't think about it, and we don't listen or apply humble inquiry—we don't think there's any need to. We don't truly get that other people's worlds are different."

It had been a full day in the living room, and it was time to wander back safely past the alligators to our cabins for a good night's sleep. I noticed the stars were out as everyone kept their flashlights shining in front of them on the trails.

NINE

Unconscious Bias

AFTER BREAKFAST WE RECONVENED IN THE LIVING room. The pancakes felt good in my belly as I settled into a different rocking chair. Normal behavior from the guys would have been to territorially stake out the same chair all week. So we required them to move around the circle and take new chairs every day for our four days together. This way they would get a new perspective, literally and metaphorically.

I was about to shift their perspective again in the next conversation. Lee was sitting to my left, with Al on the other side of him. Bill was directly across the circle. Frank strolled in while putting his phone away and sat in the last rocking chair next to Bill.

"Okay, I've got a puzzle to keep your brains working after breakfast. A young boy and his father were in a car accident. The father dies immediately at the scene. The boy is transported to the emergency room and is taken instantly into surgery, but the surgeon suddenly walks out of the operating room and says, 'I won't operate on this boy. He is my son!'"

I paused, looking around the circle at the confused faces.

"So guys, who is the surgeon?" I asked.

"Got me," said Al, as he straightened his body in his chair.

"Maybe the dad came back as a zombie?" suggested Joe.

"His stepdad?" asked Lee.

"Nope," I answered. "Frank?" I asked across the room.

Frank shrugged his shoulders.

"When I first read this puzzle I couldn't figure it out either," I said. "Nor could my teenage daughter. Sure, Lee, it could have been his stepdad. But in this case it turns out the surgeon is the boy's mother."

"Ah," said Frank. "Why didn't I think of that?"

"Good question," I answered. "Why didn't any of us think of it?"

"Because we're a bunch of white guys sitting around assuming surgeons are men," said Joe laughing.

I smiled back at Joe and explained, "The surgeon story actually refers to gender six times, with the words 'boy,' 'father,' and 'son.' There were no references to girls or mothers. This skewed reference to men reinforces any implicit bias you already had toward looking for a male in your answer."

"Makes me wonder what my unconscious assumptions are about who is a good leader," said Lee as he glanced at Joe.

"Funny you should mention that, Lee," I answered. "We can unconsciously picture white men when imagining strong leaders. Media can reinforce this. A recent cover of *Harvard Business Review* had a question in the middle of the cover. It asked "What makes a great leader?" Notably the picture behind the question was of a white male. Other factors are at play, too. For example, why is it that less than 15 percent of American men are taller than six feet, however about 60 percent of corporate CEOs are over six feet tall?" I asked.

"Sounds fishy to me," said Lee as he continued to gaze at Joe.

Joe drew back in his chair uncomfortably as he realized all eyes were on him. Al, who was one of the shortest guys in the room, had frustration written on his face.

"I feel like I am looked over or looked past regularly by taller men," said Al.

"I hear that from women frequently about their experience around men at work," added Bill.

We were examining examples of implicit or unconscious bias. The book *Blindspot* reveals that only 10 to 15 percent of Americans openly express prejudice against black Americans. However, about 75 percent of Americans display an implicit, and automatic, preference for white relative to black. Today, unconscious bias is more pervasive in the workplace than conscious bias. So what would happen if you sent the same résumés to companies with the only difference being a black-sounding name or a white-sounding name at the top? Researchers did just that. People with white-sounding names received 50 percent more callbacks for interviews than people with African American–sounding names. The very same résumés were used. Researchers calculated that a white-sounding name yields as many more callbacks as an additional eight years of experience on a résumé.

This study was duplicated with the same results in Sweden using Swedish or Middle Eastern–sounding male names. Middle Eastern candidates had a callback rate that averaged 50 percent lower. This implicit bias research is reviewed and updated yearly in a report by the Kirwan Institute. Researchers in Britain found that those with higher implicit preferences for whites compared to non-whites spend more time reviewing positive information on the white résumés and less time on the positive information on the résumés of non-white candidates. They concluded that our unconscious biases can direct our unconscious eye movements to provide precisely the information they want for a "rational" decision.

But let's say the person of color actually did get an interview callback. The implicit biases are not over. Accents and ethnic names have also been found to negatively impact an interviewer's judgment and decision to hire. In other studies, white interviewers have been found to place more physical distance between themselves and black applicants, and spend 25 percent less time with black applicants. Most of these studies find no measurable explicit bias. Rather, the bias is unconscious and can even be from people who espouse diversity.

That includes myself. I took the free ten-minute implicit bias test in Harvard's Implicit Bias website. It found I had an implicit bias toward whites and against blacks, despite the fact that I have facilitated diversity learning sessions for twenty-five years. I felt embarrassed to discover this even as I knew it wasn't my fault. I was exposed to explicit bias growing up in Iowa. For example, while in eighth grade, my sister brought home a black boy to hang out with after school. My mom later told her not to bring him home again. More universally, I grew up influenced by the media and other sources of unconscious bias that impact all of us.

I scanned the room as I shared more on race. "Studies compare homebuyers of different races, and in 8,000 cases in twenty-eight metropolitan areas, black and Asian homebuyers were told about and shown 15 to 18 percent fewer homes than white homebuyers. The same thing happens to renters. Researchers think the actual differences between races are greater than what they could measure."

"I'm not surprised," said Al. "My wife is a realtor. She was selling the house of a black family. After five months on the market someone suggested they remove any pictures and decorative items that revealed their race. The house sold in two days."

"That is startling," said Lee.

"For people of color, it can be harder to sell a house and more expensive to buy another one," I added. "One researcher examined more than two million repeat-sales housing transactions and found that blacks and Hispanics paid almost a 3-percent premium when purchasing homes."

"This is more complex than I imagined," said Frank.

"Like the exercise we did where you tried to stand up last night, Frank, this stuff has a cumulative impact on people of color," said Bill.

"It's overwhelming. But not everything is about race,"

responded Frank. "That's just going too far. I don't understand why some blacks still bring up slavery. Isn't that just reopening old wounds?"

"If you *assume* they have *negative intent* for bringing up slavery, you are going to be on the defensive," suggested Bill. "You can't magically know someone's intent. Better to stay curious and use those listening and inquiry skills. Notice, too, if you find someone who does have negative intent. Do you project that onto everyone from that group?"

I jumped in. "One of the most powerful conversations about slavery that I ever witnessed was in an Allies Lab we put on for people of all colors and genders. A white woman asked three black women why discussing slavery was so important. You could have heard a pin drop as they sat together addressing that question."

"What was their answer?" Frank asked.

"One woman said she needed to explain to her son where they came from and that slavery was where it started," I replied. "For another woman it was about claiming a strong identity coming out of surviving an astonishing ordeal. Frank, it had nothing to do with reopening old wounds. Our future-focused white male culture predisposes us not to value any revisiting of the past. But at that lab, in that instant, a powerful partnership was formed between the black women and the white woman as they discussed slavery. They were very present to each other in the moment. A year and a half later, one black woman told a conference of 800 that that conversation was the most meaningful experience of her three and a half days in the Allies Lab."

Clearly, asking a powerful question—and listening and being present for the answer—is a way to create a new partnership.

"Frank, when you heard about the slavery question, you asked how they answered. I like that you wanted to know their answers. But by jumping straight to the answers, we overlook the magic that was happening on the journey to answers. Which leads to another thought habit shift."

MINDSET #6

Focus on the present to create immediate and deeper connection—with yourself and others. Our focus is often on creating the future or examining the past while neglecting the present.

The men rocked without speaking. I purposely didn't speak to experience the silence, which is a rare occurrence in a group of white men. I noticed my own breathing. I took slower and deeper breaths. Although it was common up to that point for someone to jump in to speak, no one did. Before this, any lag in conversation was quickly filled with words. But the more time we spent together, the more the men grew comfortable with these quiet spells. The men seemed to appreciate the space to reflect.

It was December 20 a few years ago when the old Mayan calendar was ending. Some people thought that meant the world was ending. My older daughter and I were in Guatemala for a week of council and ceremony with medicine men and women from indigenous tribes who came from all over the world. My daughter was thirteen then, the youngest person in the group of about eighty. We spent most of our time that week sitting in a large circle. It was a sacred ceremony that took time to set up and consciously create. We took our turns through day and night tending the sacred fire and beating the drum in a soft heartbeat rhythm. There was plenty of time for silence. The focus was on the present. It reminded me of Quaker meetings I had attended, where one is given time to sink down inside oneself, connect to one's depth, and speak from that place. The words others spoke were powerful. Introverts had a chance to reflect and speak—they were not left behind. I felt lucky and proud that my daughter was able to witness this tradition and feel its impact.

Most executives have not experienced this powerful reference point of present-moment community connection without the distraction of a future-focused task. I glanced around the room as the white men let the silence continue, learning another way of being together. It struck me that many of the radical habits I now propose to white men were ordinary habits of traditional indigenous cultures.

My first direct taste of indigenous wisdom in the United States was in the summer after my year in South Africa. I was part of a group of Outward Bound staff invited to witness the Sun Dance ceremony on the Rosebud Reservation in South Dakota. Our main host was Albert White Hat Sr., who had recently translated the movie script *Dances with Wolves* into Lakota for the actors. Unlike many of his contemporaries who were sent to a white boarding school at age five, he didn't go until age sixteen. Thus he spoke the Lakota language and carried the stories of the elders in his village, even though they were banned. As he describes to Ken Burns in Burns's documentary, *The West*, he emerged from boarding school ashamed of his culture and who he was. White Hat personified the often-untold Native American story of our country's ethnic cleansing. Only later, in the late '60s, did he reclaim his culture and language. He became the first native Lakota speaker to publish a Lakota textbook.

Albert White Hat Sr. died a few years ago, but I remember his sense of humor and kindness to us, as well as the soul-piercing Lakota singing inside the sweat lodge. While in that lodge, I stuck my leg outside, trying to escape the unending heat. It was like an uncontrollable part of me claiming independence. I was embarrassed, but I couldn't tell if the medicine men were laughing at me, since they were speaking in Lakota and were often chuckling anyway. Either way, the humble elders always made me feel accepted. White Hat reinforced what I had learned from Nelson Mandela—to forgive and reach out to the white man with love.

Being comfortable with silence is normal for many cultures but is often a radical act for white men, especially business leaders. I glanced around the room wondering who was enjoying it and who was finding it painfully awkward. I was surprised to see Frank's face relaxed. Lee, the group's strong introvert, looked like he was in heaven.

"I'm ready to move on," said Joe.

I smiled, knowing we had stretched the group's ability to tolerate complete quiet, but it had reached its limit.

[T E N]

An Unexpected Visitor

OUR SILENCE WAS FURTHER INTERRUPTED BY AN older man who came to the door. He stood, staring at us all.

"Excuse me," he said. "I'm the general manager here at the conference center. I wanted to let you know that I just learned that there is a local investigative television reporter and a cameraman on their way to crash your meeting. They called a few minutes ago asking for directions. I just wanted to give you a heads-up."

The men gave each other bewildered looks. I stood up.

"I heard there'd been newspaper reports, but I hoped it wouldn't come to this," I said.

"Did you do something we should know about?" asked Lee with eyebrows raised over his glasses.

I actually was not surprised. Television reporters had visited us before, when we held a White Men's Caucus for the mayor of Portland, the police chief, and fourteen of their staff members. The caucus was not a secret, and its cost was part of the public record. A Portland television station sent a crew on our last day, following weeks of TV reports suggesting that the caucus was merely an excuse for a golf vacation.

We have been running corporate caucuses for almost twenty years. Yet police and government officials, who need the training just as much as the private sector, are often suspected of wasting taxpayers' money.

Joe let out a big sigh that got the guys' attention. "Look guys, they're here for me," said Joe.

Frank seemed upset. "You tell them to go away. They can't just come in here. What the hell is this—some kind of circus?"

"I don't think my company wants me to show up on TV at a gathering of white men," said Lee tensely.

It was an understandable concern. A group of white men sitting around in a business meeting would be a pretty normal scenario, but a bunch of guys in a circle of rocking chairs? Not so much.

"It's not illegal," said Al.

"Maybe they think we're wearing white robes," said Frank, with disgust in his voice.

Bill leaned in. "Tell us more, Joe," he said.

"There's been provocative press all week here in the Houston area about taxpayer money being spent on a white male–only diversity training. They've stirred up public outcry on the newspaper's weblog and Facebook page."

I first witnessed this extra-public critique almost fifteen years ago when Paul Kirkwold, the Ramsey County Manager in St. Paul, Minnesota, went before the elected county commissioners to explain sending his white male department leaders to a White Men's Caucus. I have learned to appreciate the extra courage required of public leaders who risk faulty public perception when they are proactive around issues of white men and diversity. And I remember hearing how after the caucus, Paul's female staff shed tears of gratitude as he shared his deep learning. They could feel how much he got what their experience was like as women. For years, Paul's group of white male leaders met monthly on their own initiative to continue to challenge themselves to be full diversity partners. These heartfelt stories of impact often don't make it into the press.

"What have been some of the complaints on the blog, Joe?" asked Bill.

"They think the fact that it's white males is divisive and only making things worse. Some assume it's all about blaming the white guy," Joe said.

He then reached into his bag. "Here are a few of the comments my office faxed me," he said.

He passed me the sheet of comments, and I read them out loud.

WEBLOG COMMENTS

▶ As a Caucasian male, I would like to extend my apology for anything and everything wrong in this country. I can only speak for myself, and like half of the stuff I apologize for to my wife, I really don't know what I did—but since everyone hates me, it is obvious I did something, so for these things, I am sorry. There. Now I don't need to go to this training session.

► Maybe he needs to learn this is America—we are all the same!

► Nothing racist about this at all. . . . Oh, now I see, is it so white straight males can come to understand why "minorities" need a leg up in life, are allowed more excuses as to why they can't or shouldn't be able to perform as well, and that it's really all the white males' fault. It's not like white straight males are discriminated against due to Affirmative Action. Someone should have 10x chance at a job because they are not straight white males.

► Hmm . . . diversity training facilitated by whites, not people of color. How empirical! What authenticity do they bring to ethnicity?

► Did they mention in their "diversity" scam that the first Female Millionaire in America was not white? She was in fact black, and did it on her own. And who is the richest woman in America? Oprah Winfrey. So, it can be done, once.

Frank put his hands to his head. "Wow, I'm embarrassed to say this, but I could have made some of those statements a few days ago. They really don't speak to the complexity of the issues."

Bill laughed. "Those are actually gentle compared to some of the hate mail we've received over the years. We've been accused of everything, from being a politically correct wing of the Aryan Nations, to bashing white guys, to encouraging segregation of whites."

"Look guys, I'm scared," said Al. "Given all those stereotypes about this work, how are we going to explain ourselves to a TV guy who wants to stir up controversy and increase his viewership?"

Frank turned to Lee. "What do you think we should do, Lee?"

I was surprised by Frank stepping out of his normal assertive role to seek counsel from our introvert. I smiled.

Nobody spoke as Lee took off his glasses and looked back at Frank.

"This isn't a time to baffle them with intellectual dazzle. It's a time to speak from our hearts and be authentic about what we're learning and why it's important to be here," he said.

All in the room nodded.

"Okay," said Frank.

"That feels good," said Al. "Though I am still scared."

"What do you think, Joe?" I asked. "You're the one they are targeting."

Joe straightened himself in his chair.

"I think Lee's right. There's nothing here for me to hide. I'm really glad I'm here. If we don't talk to them, they'll just perpetuate their stereotypes about this session."

Joe then laid out a plan. He suggested we allow the cameraman in to shoot background footage for a few minutes. The reporting team wouldn't be allowed to directly record our private sessions. They'd show us all meeting in a simple room, not out fishing, but working hard. Then Joe would go outside and answer questions for them.

"Then maybe we should feed them to Snappy," joked Frank.

The roam roared. The tension eased momentarily.

Suddenly, the conference manager's two-way radio beeped, and a voice announced that the television crew was on the property.

"So, should I show them here?" he asked.

Joe nodded.

Suddenly Lee stood up. "I want to talk to them, too," he said.

Joe nodded to Lee with appreciation. I was struck by how all the men had come together to confront the television coverage. It was a perfect example of the next new thought habit.

MINDSET #7

Recognize we are all in this together. Discover our interdependence. Our interconnectedness is more critical to our ultimate survival as a species than any sense of independence that may resonate with you now.

I was saying this to the group just as the cameraman walked into the room. I didn't look up but continued, "Our culture's emphasis on rugged individualism can mask how interdependent we really are in today's world. This interdependence exists both on a global scale and interpersonally—with the people we work with daily. As white guys, we like our independent streaks. But, personally, I also have learned sometimes it helps to stop and ask for directions when lost."

I saw the cameraman smile.

"Ask for directions? No way," Frank said with a laugh.

"Hold on, Frank," I said, and again addressed the group. "Can any of you think of examples of our global interdependence?"

"A nuclear leak in Japan impacts how much fish we can eat from the Pacific Ocean," said Al.

Lee jumped in. "The EU doesn't want Greece to collapse financially because it will take down all of Europe," he said.

Bill leaned forward. "One time I was working with a bunch of guys from a nuclear power plant. They were about to lose their license from the Nuclear Regulatory Authority over safety violations. When they did the audits they found that the guys working at the plant didn't think they needed their buddies to follow them around to do all the safety checks. They were making mistakes—leaving doors unlocked and leaving valves open. It was an over-reliance on individualism, and a refusal to accept their interdependence."

Thinking about our global interdependence as I sat there, I remembered a phrase I have heard several times over the years. It has been sung by U2 and was used by Bill Clinton in his acceptance speech: "There is no them, only us."

I noticed Lee nodding. I then looked to the back of the room, where the cameraman had been shooting.

"Let's take a break," I said. "It's almost lunchtime."

The camera operator left the room. Lee and Joe followed. I was not far behind.

Just outside the conference building, a TV reporter stood waiting. He knew Joe, who was the local police chief. The cameraman set up his equipment, and Joe shook the reporter's hand and introduced Lee.

The reporter began his interview with a statement: "The city spent thousands of dollars so you could learn about diversity from a room full of white guys at a fishing resort. Some people are critical of that."

Joe jumped right in, "Well, of course some people are critical. I took a political risk doing this at all. But you'll notice of course from the agenda that there was no fishing involved. We've been working twelve-hour days."

"Can you justify the cost? Is it worth it?" asked the reporter.

Joe continued, "If we, at the police department, use force the wrong way and then have to pay a settlement to some victim of that force, the outlay will be many multitudes more than this investment. We need to invest in learning that will prevent such mistakes."

Lee stepped in. "As a leader in the corporate world, I see this kind of educational investment—of time and resources—as necessary to maximize productivity, promote employee retention, and help us better relate to our diverse customers."

"So what's the most important thing you are each learning here?" asked the reporter.

Lee and Joe looked at each other to see who would speak first.

Lee started, "This caucus has helped me to see the pervasive, destructive messages directed at people of color, women, and other groups. I truly did not understand the concept or impact of systemic advantage that I have as a white male in my daily life. I was not aware of the experiences of women and minorities trying to adapt in the white male culture. Now I have greater empathy for those who are not like me."

Joe took over from there. "I fix problems for people. It changed me when I realized I didn't know how to listen and consider other perspectives. I took everything personally."

Joe's and Lee's voices sounded more vulnerable than usual, and I could tell they were speaking from their hearts.

The reporter appeared to be surprised and thanked them, and the cameraman began packing up.

I was impressed with the men's reflections on camera. I wondered what, if any of it, the reporter would use. Would he just try to perpetuate the preconception of white guys being an insensitive group—out fishing and wasting money?

Down in the water off the deck I caught a glimpse of Snappy soaking up the sun and waiting for food scraps to be dropped. Then I noticed Joe walking toward the snack bar with his arm on the back of Lee's shoulder.

I was marveling at what had evolved in the last hour. Frank, the group's alpha male, had used his new listening skills to bring in the perspective of Lee, the quiet introvert. Lee then convinced Joe to speak from his heart when talking to the reporter and then also joined the effort. If the television camera had crashed our meeting on day one, I wondered how it would have gone differently. Joe would probably have been left on his own to deal with the problem of the reporter. They were all learning, as white men, that they could hold onto their traditional strengths—tenacity, quick problem solving, and so on—*and* still greatly improve their effectiveness by bringing in new skills, such as deeper listening-based collaboration and heart-connected authenticity.

ELEVEN

Wild Father at the Door

I CAUGHT UP WITH BILL IN THE LIVING ROOM AS THE men were slowly returning from lunch. We agreed it was time to shift the conversation toward a focus on gender. When gender is typically discussed, the focus is usually on women. Rarely is a gender discussion focused on men. We were about to wade into that rarely explored territory.

I said to Bill, "You should warn the conference center staff what's coming."

Bill winked at me.

Just then Frank approached us. He was fired up.

"Hey," he said. "I really wanted to join Joe in that television interview, but I couldn't without permission from corporate communications. Is there something else that I can step into? I'm getting used to doing things I've never done before."

It was refreshing to see Frank really wanting to lean in. I looked at Bill. I knew what he was thinking. Only once before had we invited a participant to co-lead a role play we were about to do. I shrugged my shoulders, while pondering the implications if we let him do this.

Bill asked Frank, "Do you really want to take a risk?"

"I'm in," Frank insisted.

Bill and I exchanged glances and assumed it was meant to be.

The rocking chairs were filling up. Bill pulled Frank aside to give him instructions while I took my seat. The guys appeared to be ready for whatever came next.

I began. "We are going to wade more fully into the topic of gender for the rest of the day. Most organizations look at gender from an incomplete view. For example, an oil company in Europe spent a whole year developing a state-of-the-art leadership development program for women. They wanted to break through the glass ceiling. In the eleventh hour, they paused and asked themselves, 'Wait a minute, why are we doing a program with just women? Maybe there is something we need to do with the *men* in how they partner with the women.' Likewise, we all need to study the male role."

Bill was still talking to Frank just outside the doorway of the meeting room. He signaled for me to go ahead. I grabbed an extra metal folding chair and put it in the middle of the room.

"We are going to consider gender from a male perspective, exploring what it means to be a man and what messages we receive around that. In this role play, Frank is going to be a dad who is just home from work and engages Bill, his ten-year-old son. This isn't meant to imply that your experience, either as a son or a father, was like this. Parts of this may become loud."

Bill came into the room and sat in the chair in the center

of the room. Behind him was a closed door that went out into the hallway. Frank was out there preparing. Bill stared about ten feet in front of him, right where Al was sitting, at an imaginary TV screen.

"Ah, cool," Bill said. "*Star Trek.*"

The men laughed softly.

Then, suddenly, *bam!* The door behind Bill flew open. Al's eyes widened and his jaw dropped. Frank's entrance was so forceful, the door frame had cracked and the handle flew across the room.

Al gasped, "Oh, shit."

Frank was now walking into the circle, calling out, "Bill, where are you?"

"Uh, in here, Dad," answered Bill, who now slouched in his chair fearfully.

I felt myself gripping my chair. Normally this role play starts with the actor's voice only slightly elevated and gradually builds. But Frank had pushed his way *through* the door, breaking it, and his first words were full blast. He was intense. All the men stopped rocking in their chairs and everyone was still.

"Just what are you doing?" screamed Frank as he stood over Bill.

"I'm, I'm, uh . . . watching TV, Dad," said Bill, with a quiver in his voice.

"Watching TV! What? Have you done your homework yet?" shrieked Frank.

"No, Dad," said Bill, looking down at the floor, avoiding eye contact, and making himself small.

"Turn off the TV!" Frank was screaming about one foot away from Bill's ear.

Frank took a big breath and pulled out a piece of paper from his pocket. He held it in front of Bill's face.

"What's this?" asked Frank.

Now Bill was shaking and his voice stuttering.

"It's, it's a report card, Dad," said Bill.

"That's right! Very good," shouted Frank. "Now what does this say?" He pointed to one word.

"Math," replied Bill.

"Yes, and what does this say next to it?" continued Frank, pointing. Frank's voice was so forceful he was almost spitting on Bill. The veins in his neck were bulging. Frank was having no difficulty in this role.

Bill struggled to speak. He was shaking.

"C, Dad—it's a C," Bill managed to speak.

Somehow Frank got even louder. "That's right—a C. And what did we say we were going to do?"

It seemed to me Frank's presence was permeating every cell in Bill's body. Like a dog with a tail between his legs, Bill shrank farther in his chair.

"B, Dad. We said we'd get a B," said Bill.

Frank became more irritated.

"And you're watching TV, not doing your homework! You're not even trying."

At this point Bill appeared to be sobbing. "I tried, Dad. I really tried," Bill mumbled, as his crying grew louder.

This enraged Frank even more. "Oh, don't cry! What kind of son are you?"

Frank pushed Bill off the chair, which bent and crumbled. Then I realized Frank had actually pushed Bill *through* the chair. Bill sobbed on the floor, his arms and legs curled into a ball.

"No son of mine is going to be a crybaby," screamed Frank as he stormed out of the room.

The rest of us sat in our chairs, dead quiet. The only sound was Bill's wailing for the next twenty seconds. Bill was lying right at the base of Joe's chair. Joe watched without moving a muscle.

I finally broke the long silence.

"Take a few minutes and talk to the man seated next to you about what came up for you as you witnessed that role play."

Bill slowly peeled himself off the floor, slightly shocked. "Wow," was all he said.

Frank wandered back into the room with a long sullen face. He sat down next to Lee, who was the only man without a partner. They started talking.

I surveyed the room: the crumpled chair and the broken door handle were on the floor, and part of the door frame was splintered open. The role play had been more intense than any I'd ever seen. I wondered how much of that was role play and how much of that was Frank.

We pulled the men back into one group conversation.

"What came up for folks?" I asked.

Thirty seconds went by. Finally Lee spoke, as he wiped a tear from behind his thick glasses. "Well, I wish that were my dad. My dad wasn't around. And when he was around, he was indifferent about everything. I don't remember him ever coming to me. I always went to him. I wish he'd cared. I would have taken anything, even if it looked like that. At least it would have been better than nothing."

The men were shocked. That was the last thing I expected to hear.

Joe leaned toward Lee, who was next to him.

"I'm sorry, Lee," said Joe. "It pains me to think you would have preferred that over what you had."

Across the circle, Al had a different response. "I *did* get that," he said. "That was essentially my dad."

I could see the pain on Al's face. He looked like he had seen a ghost.

"Are you okay?" I asked.

"I'll be fine." Al paused. "Actually, I'm not fine. That was quite an ordeal growing up. I've never actually told a soul how much physical abuse I experienced. I would sometimes provoke my father so he wouldn't go after my little brothers. He never acted that way to my sisters, but he was hard on us boys. I took the brunt of it."

No one made a sound as they took in Al's words. I was scared. I wondered if our little role play had gone too far and to what degree Al was experiencing flashbacks. One of our female colleagues has questioned whether our role playing crosses over into psychodrama. Choosing an experiential learning model, we always reach beyond the same old analytical and didactic teaching methods that white men are so used to. PowerPoint slides are not the best way to encourage deep personal growth or illustrate difficult truths. I could tell that Frank was having some emotional fallout, too. I was glad we always had a consulting psychologist available to call on during a break, should we need expert coaching. Often, our caucus explorations touched an unexpected nerve.

"Al, I heard you say that you have never told anyone before about your father's abuse. Did I hear that right?" asked Bill.

We all sat for a while waiting for Al to be able to speak. I watched his face for any sign of how he was doing.

"I hadn't thought about that for a long time," said Al. "Yes, I have never told anyone before." He seemed both relieved and nervous.

"What's it like to tell us that?" Bill asked.

"It feels like a huge load off my chest," said Al. "I'm also a bit nervous about putting it out there. What will you think of me now?" He glanced at the floor and let out a big sigh.

Frank was on the edge of his chair, leaning across the circle toward Al.

"Al, we have known each other for a long time," said Frank. "Knowing this about you has me caring about you even more. I am really proud that you survived what you endured."

Al seemed surprised at Frank's loving response. He relaxed and dropped his shoulders. I was also happily surprised to see this softer side of Frank, and I was relieved to know Al felt comforted.

There was a sweet peace in the group as everyone took in this tender exchange.

Tearing up, Frank started to speak but had to pause to regain his composure. "What I did to Bill in that role play . . ." Frank paused, struggling to keep talking. "What I did . . . is how I am with my son."

Frank solemnly gazed at the different faces in the room. "I never really saw the intensity of how I am. Until now," he said.

No one in the group moved or spoke. All eyes were on Frank. There was a heartfelt presence in the room in response to his courage in speaking his truth. No one rushed in to problem-solve or fix anything. We were in a space of just *being* with him versus *doing* something or fixing him. Without talking about it, the group had shifted into a new radical thought habit.

MINDSET #8

Explore just *being*, and step out of *doing*. We often assume our essential value comes from focusing on action and getting things done. But acting without reflection can derail success. New paths open when we take the time to just *be*.

At that point I could have presented a new radical thought habit around *being* versus *doing*, but I didn't want to take away from the emotional power of the moment. It was an intense time for Frank; he was seeing himself mirrored in the role play. He also saw the potential impact on his son, having heard how it affected his longtime colleague Al.

"Frank, how you just spoke to Al is how I really wanted

my dad to be with me," said Lee. Frank's face lightened for a second, then grew sad again.

"I don't know how to be gentle like that," said Frank. "I just seem to always be hard on him."

"Was that how your dad was to you?" asked Joe, who had been quietly listening.

"Yes," replied Frank.

I noticed Lee fidgeting in his chair.

"That harshness doesn't have to be what you pass on," said Lee. "Stop using your old habit. Or, more accurately, your dad's habit."

Frank looked at Lee with interest as Lee continued.

"I am determined to not pass on to my kids the lack of attention I received from my dad. They've had a different experience handed down, and your son can too. It's not too late."

"Frank," I said, "what I appreciate right now is your wanting to be different. You don't need to know how you are going to do it. I have no doubt you will find a way."

Bill had been unusually silent all this time. He finally spoke up.

"The first time we held this caucus, I knew I wanted to put myself in a situation where I couldn't just hide out as a neutral facilitator. So I invited my dad, and he came. He actually came to three different caucuses in the early days."

The guys looked surprised by Bill's revelation.

"What was that like?" asked Frank.

"It was great. He really showed up. It was certainly an

advantage to have him in the caucus. He had a short temper at times when I was a kid. We talked about that. Going through these discussions together really touched us both."

If we were going to truly explore gender, it was important to reflect on some of our original messages around manhood. For most men, it starts with their fathers.

I fondly remembered Bill's dad with the caucus when the conversation felt too intellectual or too touchy-feely. He often yelled out, "Bullshit!"

I also thought about my dad, who is 97. He was never overbearing like Frank was in the role play—I got that from my mom. My dad was not absent like Lee's dad, though he was passive to some degree. I also learned from him how to be both mellow and passive. I've had to learn to assert my voice and authority in the world. On the other hand, my dad was always around and would respond to my requests for help and support if I sought him out. I like knowing that the playful humor and patience I leverage in my work and life I learned from my dad. I carry all that forward to my daughters with active engagement.

The role play, while risky, was effective. The next step was to keep an eye on Frank and Al, and connect the role play to gender insights in our lives. And, of course, to repair the damage to the door.

[TWELVE]

Act like a Man

TWENTY MINUTES LATER, THE DOOR WAS FIXED. THE guys, on their own initiative, had run out to their trucks and cars to grab tools during the break and put everything back together. The chair, of course, was crumbled beyond repair, and we would need to speak to the conference center about that. The guys and their tools had taken care of everything else.

"Would you say that being a man includes being able to fix stuff?" asked Bill as he gazed at the repaired door. He then laughed. "Nice work," he said.

"Hey, what about the chair, guys?" I asked with a teasing tone. The chair still lay in a heap in the corner of the room.

"A strength overused is a weakness, remember?" Joe said, winking at me.

Following up on the role play we had just done, we were about to explore more specifically the messages we received around what it means to act like a man.

Bill stepped up to a flipchart with a marker. "I want you all to describe the messages you've received in your lifetime about what it means to be a man," Bill said.

"Be tough," said Frank.

"Don't cry," said Al. He let out a sigh. He looked like he was still processing the role play.

"Not only no crying," added Lee, "but don't show *any* pain or weakness."

Joe spoke up, "Yes, no vulnerability. Have it all together. Always know the answers."

"Actually we have a name for that," answered Bill. "We call it Acquired Male Answer Syndrome."

"What's that?" asked Joe.

"When asked a definitive question, give a definitive answer, whether you know what the hell you are talking about or not," said Bill.

The guys roared.

"I do that," said Frank.

"We know," said Lee, glancing over at Frank.

"What else?" asked Bill.

"Be a provider," added Al.

"Hey, what about our possessions?" asked Joe. "Have lots of stuff."

"Have a big car," added Lee.

"Or a big hard drive," said Joe.

"Well, have something big!" said Frank. The guys were chuckling.

"Another message is to play sports and be able to talk sports," said Al.

"And win at all costs," said Bill.

"Hold your liquor," I added.

"Actually, the first time I came home from college, my dad put a bottle of whiskey on the table with two glasses and said 'I don't trust a man who doesn't drink with me,'" said Bill.

"What did you do?" asked Joe.

"I refused to drink. I just didn't want to," said Bill. "My younger brother had a more fascinating response. When my dad said the same thing to him, he stared back at him and said 'I never trust a man who doesn't smoke weed with me.'"

The men laughed.

"It was like two generations of men staring each other down across the table," said Bill.

I smiled, appreciating the rebel character in his brother, who recently had begun facilitating our caucuses.

"Any other messages stand out for acting like a man?" asked Bill.

"Don't ask for directions," said Lee.

"Don't dance," said Al.

"How about PCI?" asked Joe.

"What's PCI?" I asked.

"Piston Cylinder Index," said Joe. "You count up the number of pistons in your cars and power tools and compare it to the other guys.'"

The group roared in laughter. Clearly Joe had struck a nerve.

"I bet I would beat all you guys," Joe added.

"What are you noticing about these messages?" Bill asked, ignoring Joe's challenge.

"Basically, be tough and show no chinks in the armor," said Frank.

"My brothers pretty much drilled that message into me,"

said Joe. "I was once locked in a wooden toy chest for seven hours. I was the youngest of seven brothers."

"Wow," I said. "That sounds terrifying. I bet you still don't like tiny spaces."

"Nope," said Joe. "I still get claustrophobic."

"There is actually a hockey coach in Minnesota who purposely recruits boys with older brothers because he thinks they are tougher," I added.

"Well, it's true," replied Joe.

"We also downplay pain or being hurt," said Bill. "Once I was on the top of a ladder, and it slid out away from the side of my house, and I rode the ladder down from the third story. For months I ignored what I eventually found out was a broken toe."

I added, "We also have a colleague who had a lump in his throat that he ignored for more than two years before going in and finding out he had throat cancer. Our focus on toughness and ignoring pain can have life-threatening consequences."

"How do these messages connect to you, Frank, and how you saw yourself acting in the father-son role play?" I asked. The group paused, knowing that was likely to be an emotional question for Frank.

"Oh, this was just getting fun, but now you're going to make it all personal?" quipped Frank.

I didn't answer, and he paused. During the silence I imagined a lump growing in his throat.

"It absolutely connects. A lot of these messages describe my behavior," Frank said. "But in my toughening up my son, he doesn't want anything to do with me." Frank looked at Al, who had the abusive father.

"If your son's hurting, you don't seem to want to know it," said Lee.

Frank looked at the floor. "I guess that's true. He did come home from school last week in tears, telling me the other boys were bullying him. I told him to suck it up and not to cry about it. It seemed like the right thing to do at the time."

Al spoke up. "Frank, what I most wanted from my dad in times like that was to know that he loved me and it would all be okay. I wanted him to know what I was feeling. I didn't want him to shut me down or get mad at me."

Al and Frank stared at each other.

"What I got instead from my dad was what you modeled in the role play. I felt very alone and afraid," Al said.

I noticed tears in Frank's eyes.

"Frank's being emotional right now," I said. "Does anyone here feel like we should tell Frank to suck it up?"

The guys shook their heads no. In fact, the men seemed to appreciate Frank's honesty and vulnerability.

"Frank," said Al, "we've had our offices next to each other for twenty years. You know, I never knew you went through a divorce until one day that picture disappeared from your desk."

Frank swallowed hard. "That was the most painful thing I've ever dealt with in my life, and I never told another man at work."

All the other men in the room were leaning forward in

their rocking chairs, watching this interaction between the two co-workers.

Al clearly wanted to speak but had gotten choked up. The group waited several minutes. When he could talk, what he said was equally surprising.

"I have to tell you all something. I've been treated for clinical depression the past two years," said Al. "I've never told another soul, let alone another man at work. I was afraid people would think I wasn't ready for that next promotion."

The men were shocked at what was being shared in the room. The masks were coming off, and Al and Frank, long-time colleagues, were getting real. The price men pay for hiding their vulnerability is not receiving support from their male colleagues. We've learned to hide behind the armor, which feels safe but creates a lonely jail.

In our white male culture, we define much of our identity by what we do in our jobs. So when we know each other's jobs, we think we know each other. Our curiosity often stops there. As a contrast, in some cultures, such as can be found in Mexico, men don't work together until they've gotten to know each other, and sometimes, even their families become close. That's exactly the reason why, in the beginning of the caucus, we never have the guys introduce themselves by job title; this creates space for connecting in a new way. In our white male culture, we usually build relationships only when it's pragmatically required to accomplish our jobs. One impact is that white men are rarely vulnerable with each other in a way that creates true emotional support. Even if one shares, the other may not be able to reciprocate, and the whole interaction can regress to banter. Our struggles remain isolated behind a wall of belief that work and personal life are separate—and never the twain shall meet. Frank and Al broke that wall that day, a wall that had existed for twenty years.

"You guys are modeling another radical habit shift for white men," I said.

> **MINDSET #9**
>
> Show up with vulnerability—it's a form of courage. You'll create more openness and deeper connections than ever before.

Brené Brown has authored several books and presented a popular TED Talk on vulnerability. She says that vulnerability is the purest form of courage. That is a much different perspective on courage than the Rambo or Braveheart charge-into-battle model of courage.

Frank and Al's interaction reflected this exactly.

"How are the rest of you being impacted by the conversation between Frank and Al?" I asked.

Lee leaned forward. "I don't have many close male friends I share deeply with, and I think that is common. I wish I had a connection with other men like you two have," he said.

Joe paused and buried his face in his hands for a short time. He looked like he was about to say something but then stopped.

"Anything else, Joe?" asked Bill.

"No," responded Joe.

There was a brief pause. Bill and I looked at each other.

Bill continued to speak, "We've identified messages boys and men receive around what it means to act like a man. Frank summarized it as 'be tough and show no chinks in the armor.' So what happens to boys and men when they don't fit this model? What do you get called?"

The words came fast from all around the room. I lost track of who said what.

I heard "wimp," "wuss," "softie," "girly man," "weak," "sissy," "queer," "fag," "homo," "mamma's boy," "dickless," and "lame."

"That was easy," Bill said. "What's the general theme?"

Frank jumped in. "Well, basically you're either feminine or gay."

"That's right," continued Bill. "Our behavior is in part controlled by our fear of being labeled a woman or gay by our male peers. I remember when I was growing up on the playground, I didn't even know what 'fag' or 'homo' meant—I just knew they were bad."

Lee was nodding.

"So we learn to suppress or hide anything others might identify as being feminine or as potentially homosexual. If we do show it, we might get kicked out of the guys' club or pushed down in status." I added, "This reinforces the tenets of white male culture: be the rugged individual, don't ask for help and don't say 'I don't know,' stay rational and don't show emotion, focus on action, limit personal sharing or reflection, pay attention to status and rank, and opt for playful banter over deep connection."

"My dad was a World War II vet," said Lee. "He never ever talked about it. He was in very dangerous, terrifying situations. I only heard about it from others."

"Most of us men hide both physical pain and emotional pain from others," said Bill. "We hide our incompetency too, for fear of embarrassment."

I knew this myself too well. In elementary school, I grew up having trouble peeing in front of other boys in the bathroom. It was embarrassing to not be able to go when I had to or wanted to. I would often go into a stall to avoid the embarrassment. I was constantly worried about being discovered standing there not being able to pee and being teased. I dreaded going to the bathroom. I lived with it, and it constantly put me in touch with social vulnerability and humiliation. This continued into my college days. I went to the counseling center where I learned to relax using biofeedback. As an adult I finally realized this was fairly common and is called *paruresis*. Given our rugged individualist don't-show-weakness mode, many of us who struggle with such vulnerability don't realize we are not alone.

I looked around the room at the men in rocking chairs as the afternoon wore on. They didn't realize it, but they were rocking in sync again.

I told the group about the time we worked with a leadership team from an engineering company who was attending a White Men's Caucus together. As soon as they sat down as a group they started zinging each other. It was rapid fire, dishing out the crap onto each other. They had their own word for it—they called it "smack talk." It included terms of endearment for each other and constant ribbing. It was what I often observe, only turned up to a high frequency and volume. Partway through the caucus they said that women and people of color come into their team meetings and feel uncomfortable with the dynamic—except for a few women who could dish it out better than they could—but they'd had to learn smack talk in order to belong. Then one white guy actually admitted that he didn't like it because he wasn't that good at it.

I paused and noticed the men nodding.

"I'm not very good at smack talk either," said Al. "But at least when you get the ribbing from others, you know you belong. It's better than getting nothing."

"It is a way we connect and bond," said Bill. "But if it's the only way to connect and bond, there isn't room for deeper connection."

"I'm tired of the shallowness of just bantering," said Al. "I want to just be myself and bring both my tenacity and my vulnerability."

"I want that, too," said Frank. "For you, for me, and for my son."

The men were exploring how vulnerability was truly a strength rather than a weakness. It had been a full afternoon. Time for a well-deserved two-hour break before dinner.

THIRTEEN

Bringing the Heart

DURING THE BREAK, I WENT OUT FOR A RUN AND NO-
ticed Frank and Al sitting on the deck talking. I later realized
they had talked straight through the two-hour afternoon
break as if they had each found a long lost friend. When
they didn't show up for dinner, I spotted them outside on
the deck still talking, right above Snappy, who was probably
hoping for some treats. I was sure they weren't engaged in
the typical guy talk about sports, weather, or hobbies. At
the very end of dinner they came in to get some food, then
returned to the deck to continue their talk.

When the men finally reassembled in the living room, I
called Frank and Al in from the deck. They looked refreshed
as they entered the room.

"Any reflections come up for folks over our break time?"
Bill asked the group.

Joe was eager to speak. "I shared something with Lee at
dinner, and he encouraged me to bring it here." Emotion
was evident on his face. All the men waited quietly. I suspected this was what Joe had been thinking about earlier in
the afternoon.

"My eight-year-old son has a rare condition," Joe said. His eyes were soft. "He was only expected to live another year, and we are halfway through that year." He paused. "Every day is precious."

I heard a few gasps and moans of reaction. The guys were in shock. I felt all my thoughts and worries melt away inside me as I listened to another man speak about what really mattered. It was as if the whole room dropped from the head level down to the heart level in one breath. Suddenly all the lighter dinner conversations seemed insignificant and even a distraction. Why do we spend so much time speaking to each other on a surface level when there is so much at the heart level where we can connect? Why do we rarely go there unless encouraged or when we stumble into deep sharing almost by accident?

"How are you doing right now?" asked Lee.

"It's actually good to talk about this. It's been a tough journey. My family time is priceless," replied Joe.

"How is your son doing?" asked Bill.

Joe looked up and around the room for the first time.

"He is taking it very well. I'm so proud of him. He is my knight in shining armor," said Joe.

"I'm sure glad he has you for a father," said Frank. "You are obviously there for him."

"I'm glad you're his dad too," said Lee as he stared at Joe.

Joe was visually moved by Frank's and Lee's comments. His body relaxed.

"I wasn't always there," said Joe. "My career pulled me away for long hours. I felt like I was always on. Eventually, as a police sergeant, I learned to put my smartphone in the gun safe along with my gun when I arrived home. If there was an emergency they knew how to call my home line."

"That was a good idea," said Lee. The other men nodded.

Frank shook his head. "As a corporate executive, I couldn't do that today," said Frank. "I'm expected to be available 24/7."

"But we're the leaders in our company, Frank," said Al. "If we don't model work and life balance, who will? Everyone follows our example."

"Yeah, you're right," said Frank. "I didn't say I liked it." Frank seemed to appreciate Al's challenge.

Al continued. "I know. I've paid a heavy price. In my previous job I almost lost my marriage."

"Tell them what you told me during the dinner break," Frank ordered.

The men looked at Al expectantly.

"I used to do whatever my old company wanted. At the drop of a hat I would go across the world when they needed me," Al said. "Once they asked me on a Thursday to go to Singapore on Friday—the next day."

"Did you?" asked Lee.

"I told them my son had a soccer game that weekend. Well, they said I wasn't a team player."

"So, did you go?" Lee asked again.

"Yep. When I got back, no one was home. Those were the days before cell phones. I went over to the neighbors to see if my wife and kids were there. They hadn't seen them. I called our friends. I almost called the police. Eventually I found them 1,000 miles away in Chicago. They were all at my mother-in-law's home. My wife said she had had it with my being gone. I don't blame her. I worked and traveled so much, I hadn't set foot in my son's school in years. I thought my job was always at stake. My son's teacher didn't even know he had a dad."

"So, you're still married? What did you do after you found out she was staying at her parents?" probed Joe sympathetically.

"Her parents were great," said Al. "They took the kids for a few days so we could go off and have a heart-to-heart. I committed to really being home. I had to choose. I didn't want to lose her. And I realized my kids deserved more."

"So, what did your company do then?" I asked.

"Oh, I quit. That's when I came to work where I do now. They never would have accepted my family focus. That culture was crazy. I even left on business trips the day after my children were born. I was so obsessed with proving my allegiance to the company, often my wife would help me drop my car off in the company parking lot on Saturday so it looked like I was at work on the weekend. Everyone did that."

"That reminds me of when I was working in the Pentagon. Some of the generals used to order two military caps so they could keep one sitting on their desk, so it looked like they were always there," said Frank.

"Wow," I said. "What a game. Reminds me of a friend of mine who has lived the last thirty years in a remote log cabin in the northern Minnesota wilderness. He once joked to me, 'You know what the trouble with the rat race is? Even if you win—you're still a rat.'"

The men laughed. It was so true. What race are we trying to win anyway?

Sometimes it takes a wake-up call. I told the men of an often-traveling sales executive I knew who was at home cooking pancakes when his toddler tugged on his pants and asked, "Daddy, do you live here?" His son didn't even know he lived at home. It shocked him. He vowed to be home significantly more. Another friend stayed home more after noticing his kids were starting to behave like their nanny. He realized he wanted to be more of their role model than the nanny was.

Frank then pointed out that our children's generation is actually repelled by the work habits of their fathers' generation. "My oldest son was certainly impacted by what he saw in me growing up," he said. "He just finished college in engineering. I suggested he apply to work in my company. I was startled at his answer. He said, 'Dad, I would never work for that company. I saw what they did to you. You worked constantly when I was growing up. You weren't around.'"

I listened intensely. I wondered what my daughters would say about me. Have I done better? Since my divorce eight years ago, I've arranged to be home every other week, to be present on those weeks when my daughters are with me. Lately they have been with me much more than half-time. I already feel the time is precious with my older daughter, who is less than two years away from finishing high school. We have had years of adventurous spring break trips and rituals like Sunday skiing and summer camping in the local lookout tower. We love our time together. My friends have noticed this and commented on it. If I were a mom, however, this close connection would probably not be anything unusual. As a father, it's praiseworthy.

My daughters and I have a red bound book that is an ongoing journal of our adventures and our funny moments. What I always ask for on my birthday and Christmas is for them to write in the journal so we can all read and remember our collective stories when we are older. Whenever something funny happens in everyday life, one of them will say, "We better write that in the red journal." I actually started a separate journal for each of them when they were born. But there are only about six pages written in each. Somehow they got put aside during the hectic early years. I want to get back to each of them and fill in those missing years. Will I actually make that happen? Or will I let the time escape me? Time is a limited currency just like money. I want to feel good about how I spent my time when I look back on my life.

Richard Leider, the author of nine books, was the original creator of the Life Career Renewal courses I taught in the wilderness at the Voyageur Outward Bound School. I really enjoyed leading those courses. Over Richard's career he has interviewed thousands of seniors about what they would have done differently in their lives. He always finds three themes. First, they would hit the pause button and be more *reflective*. Second, they would be more *courageous* in sharing their voice and authenticity. Third, they would make sure their lives mattered—that they *made a difference* in the world. Most of us on our deathbeds will not wish we had worked more and spent less time with our families. Yet the cultural treadmill many white men are sprinting on pulls them out of work/life balance at the expense of themselves and those close to them.

I saw Bill begin to speak.

"My family teases me that according to my astrological chart I was born in the house of work. I live and breathe my work every day. It's my passion. I regularly have to take trips out of the country with my wife and occasionally other family members in order to slow down and reflect."

I knew this to be true. He was on the road most weeks. Bill's pace made me look like a lazy white guy. Yet I had recently seen him make shifts to be home more with his wife. Their trips around the globe are remarkable because of their spontaneity, often connecting them with families in remote corners of the world.

"How else does this work/family/life struggle for balance play out at work for you guys?" I asked the group.

"I leave work early every Thursday to coach my son's little league team," said Lee.

"Do you catch any flack for that?" asked Bill.

"Not anymore," replied Lee. "I did at first. But I didn't let that stop me."

"I wish I had done that," said Al.

"You're too focused on wanting other guys' approval, Al," Frank blurted out. Frank had been softening, and this felt like a return to his former tough self. "I want you to not care about what others think and do what you want. To hell with them," said Frank.

Al was nodding as he wiped a tear. Clearly Frank had struck a nerve.

"Thanks, Frank," said Al. "It's true. Actually I needed to hear that."

We were continuing to see the fruits of Al and Frank's deepening connection. They were both more comfortable challenging each other as a way to support each other. It reminded me of the same dynamic I see in my men's group at home in Sandpoint, Idaho, which has been going for over ten years and recently was the subject of a documentary called *About Men*. I was glad they were beginning to gain the deeper support I have enjoyed in my life for years. The men in my men's group know me well and don't let me get away with falling asleep on my growth journey. I wish all men could have that level of support and healthy challenge in their life.

Joe began to speak. "I took my job as police chief on the condition that I would be home every weekend. Only in a rare community emergency do I violate that condition."

"That's impressive," said Lee. "As I said before, we have to lead in this arena. Others, including other white guys, will follow our lead."

A 2013 Pew Research study on working families found that 46 percent of fathers report they don't think they spend enough time with their children, versus 23 percent of mothers. Clearly there is room for a shift. Indeed, I once had the opportunity to present at a conference in San Francisco. At first I thought I couldn't do it because I had my daughters during that time. Then I realized I could do both. So I took my daughters on a vacation, first to L.A., where we did the usual Hollywood tour and walked Venice Beach. We even went to a Taylor Swift concert—me and 13,000 screaming girls. We eventually drove in a rented convertible up the coast to San Francisco. The next day, on the spur of the moment, I took my daughters into my conference session. They sat behind me. It was the first time they had gotten to see me in any professional setting. Halfway through, they had had enough and decided to return to the hotel room. I then owned up to the group that what I had just done was, in fact, an example of male privilege. People saw me as a dedicated family man, but if I were a woman presenter who had brought her kids with her, I most likely would have had my professional competence questioned. One man in the audience said he was glad I had brought them because it would make it easier for others to do the same in the future. It was one of those instances when I actually did recognize my privilege at the time, which is often not the case.

Most men don't even know what balance is. The old adage is: my dad was a real man—he worked till the day he died. Companies used to give men awards for never taking any of their sick days.

Lee was continuing his conversation. "As leaders, do you answer emails on weekends? If you do, chances are your subordinates feel an obligation to do the same."

Frank looked at Lee across the circle. "I do because my staff tells me they don't want a barrage of emails Sunday night or Monday morning. But they are always answering them when I send them."

"Figure out a different way, Frank," Al said.

Frank smiled. "I'm not sure I like this new challenging friend style."

"Too bad," replied Al.

"Any other suggestions, Lee?" I asked.

"Take vacations. Disconnect from the office. You need the break and your staff does too," continued Lee.

No one protested this time.

"There is one thing I want to point out to you all about our conversation since dinner," I said. "I am appreciating the level of heart in the room. The Chinese symbol for consensus literally means the head and heart come together and speak with one voice. It can be a *both/and* versus assuming we must choose rationality or emotion."

Our white male culture assumes we can't contain both. The group was experiencing a heartful way of sharing that many had never before experienced among men. This important Leadership Skill of Integrating Head and Heart is critical for success both in and out of the workplace. Not everyone in our lives resonates at the head level; some are moved by more heartful expression. Research shows EQ, or emotional intelligence, is more critical for leaders' success than either IQ or technical skills. But the white male culture does not emphasis EQ, and promotions are still often based on IQ or technical skills.

FOURTEEN

Getting the World That Women Live In

THERE WAS STILL MUCH TO COVER WEDNESDAY EVEning, our final evening, regarding gender. We had thus far successfully started a gender conversation with a focus on exploring our assumptions and behavior as men. Now it was time to expand our focus and compare our world as men to the world that women navigate every day. Despite the full day and long hours, the group seemed ready to dive in. I nodded at Bill, and he began to speak.

"This afternoon we studied the messages we receive as boys and men around what it means to act like a man. Now let's start with looking at some of the messages girls and women receive, specifically at a subset of messages around what it means to 'act like a lady' in society, and then we'll get into work issues for women."

I stepped up to a flipchart to capture what was about to happen.

"Be prim and proper," stated Lee.

"Cross your legs," said Al.

Frank sat quietly pondering for a minute.

"Okay," said Joe. "Be social. Remember birthdays and anniversaries."

"Be kind, graceful," said Frank.

"Smile," I added.

"Really?" asked Frank looking at me.

"Yeah," I said. "People go up to girls or women in public and tell them to smile. Has that ever happened to you?"

"Never," said Frank.

"Smile," said Al jokingly to Frank.

Frank just glared at Al. He did not smile back.

"Let the man drive the car," said Al.

"Yep, defer to your man," added Bill. "And how about this: feel men's feelings for them."

"Take care of the kids," said Lee. "Cook and clean."

"Don't have bodily noises or odors," said Frank.

The men were surprised how quickly the messages came out.

"Let's hit the pause button," said Bill. "What are some words girls and women are called when they don't align with those messages? Permission granted to be graphic for a moment."

The words again came fast from around the room. I heard "tramp," "butch," "lesbo," "femi-nazi," "heifer," and "bitch."

"Let's stand back and compare these messages to those messages around acting like a man that we brainstormed before dinner," I said. A few noiseless seconds passed as the men glanced between the two charts.

"The traits in the two lists seem opposing," said Joe. "You're either one or the other."

"The consequences of not conforming are also harsh," said Lee. "To not fit those messages around acting like a lady means being called a man hater, a homosexual, or even an animal."

"These messages are 90 percent similar across age groups and race in my experience over twenty years," said Bill. "So what if we created a third list of the traits of a good leader in your organization. What list would it be closer to?"

Frank jumped in, "It would be closer to the man list. You've got to be tough and get results."

"I think some of the lady list is starting to be valued for leadership," said Lee, "like empathy and relating skills."

"But if you are a guy and you take on too much empathy and emotion, what happens?" I asked.

"That's easy," said Al. "I get called touchy-feely."

"Yes," I responded. "Now if a leader is identified more by the act-like-a-man list, what happens for women who are leaders?"

The men pondered the question for a moment.

"What I see," said Lee, "is that if women take on too many of the act-like-a-man traits, they are bumped off the act-like-a-lady list."

"That's true," said Bill. "Women are in a double bind. They struggle to be tough or assertive and *nice* at the same time. As men, we just get to be assertive."

"Which is why men can be seen as assertive but women who exhibit the same behavior can be described as bitches," I added.

As the men considered this dilemma, I recalled Catalyst's

report, "The Double-Bind Dilemma for Women in Leadership." The report confirms what we were just exploring. Catalyst studied perceptions of more than a thousand leaders from across Europe and the United States and identified three predicaments. The first is called Extreme Perceptions—too soft, too tough, and never just right. In fact, when women act consistent with gender stereotypes, they are viewed as less competent leaders (too soft). When women act in ways inconsistent with such stereotypes, they're considered unfeminine (too tough). The second predicament is the High Competence Threshold—female leaders face higher standards and lower rewards than male leaders. They have to prove over and over again that they can lead and manage others' stereotypical expectations constantly. The third predicament is called Competent but Disliked—as leaders, women are perceived as either competent or likable, but rarely both.

For many of the men, this whole complex maze of double binds was new terrain to comprehend. Lee appeared solemn—his face was flushed and he was rocking slowly and deeply back and forth. Joe noticed too, and we both watched him expectantly.

"Lee," I said, "you seem to be pondering something."

"The glass ceiling was never real to me until my older daughter told me it was," said Lee. "She was working at one of the big accounting firms in New York. She knew she was getting less money than her male colleagues for the same job. She was not getting promoted. She felt so much pressure to work long hours and perform with no room for mistakes." He paused to survey his audience.

"You look quite sad," said Joe.

"I am sad," answered Lee. "I couldn't protect her from that harsh environment."

The men patiently listened to Lee. Though he was often quiet, they had learned that Lee was a rich source of wisdom.

He continued, "One boss said to her 'If you want to be a partner, you need to dress like a partner.' And then he pointed out the senior executive women. Well, all the senior partners wore St. John suits, a brand a lot of women executives wear that is very expensive. The female execs also had clothing consultants to help them get it perfect. How my daughter dressed was constantly scrutinized, and she couldn't afford the clothes they told her to wear." Lee watched Joe as he continued. "You and I, as guys, we can wake up, throw on a basic pair of khakis and a button-down shirt, and we're seen as competent."

Joe nodded.

"For my daughter, it was always an early morning wake-up and two hours to do hair and dress and be ready for work," Lee explained.

"I'm tired just *hearing* about it," said Frank. "I remember a female executive who called me for advice on what kind of shoes to wear while visiting a navy ship. I've never had to sort out what shoes were appropriate for me to wear on a ship."

"Your daughter's life sounds complex, Lee," said Al.

"That's just the beginning, guys," said Lee. "She learned golf just to fit in and be able to have the social access time with the guys."

"So did I," said Al.

Lee was on an unusual roll. "And she learned to talk sports, even though she could care less. But the guys would still go to games at the company's pro basketball arena and not think to invite her. They also wouldn't invite her out to lunches, but they would go out with each other all the time. She finally asked one of the guys she knew best why she was excluded and found out some were afraid of what their wives would think if they went out to lunch with a young woman colleague."

"That sounds lonely, Lee," said Joe.

Much of this Bill and I had heard over the years, mostly from women and occasionally from guys who had women in their lives impacted by these dynamics. Research has also illuminated these challenges. The latest research shows women are paid 78 cents for every dollar men are paid, even though we have had fifty years of equal-pay laws. But most of us white males want to believe the playing field is level and that these inequities, barriers, and double standards don't exist. We notice the progress that has been made but don't see the vast gaps that remain. From our perspective, believing there's a level playing field, we might blame women and say they just need to lean in and try harder. For example, research shows that women don't ask for raises as much as men do. A recent survey of 2,000 men and women found 39 percent of women said they asked for a higher salary when starting a new job, compared to 54 percent of men. The same survey said that 75 percent of women do get more money when they ask for it. So you might say it's a woman's fault for not asking for more money and that women need to change. But other studies show that women who do ask for money are seen more negatively than men who ask for more money. The double binds are at play.

But there is more. Implicit bias is also a factor. In one study conducted in 2014, researchers sent emails to 6,500 randomly selected professors at 259 American universities. Each email was from a fictional, prospective out-of-town student expressing interest in the professor's doctorate program and seeking guidance. The emails were identical except they were from twenty different senders, whose names represented ten different race or gender categories. Professors were more responsive to white male students than to female, black, Hispanic, Indian, or Chinese students in almost every discipline. In business schools, 87 percent of white males received a response compared to just 62 percent of all females and minorities combined. That's a 25 percent gap in response rate simply by changing the name on the emails.

Another study sent the same one-page summary of qualifications for a lab director job to professors of biology, chemistry, and physics at three public and three private universities. Half of the emails were from an applicant named John and half were from an applicant named Jennifer. Scientists rated the male student more competent, more likely to be hired, deserving of a better salary, and worth spending more time mentoring. The gaps were significant. The professors were asked to rate the applicant on a scale of 1 to 7 and suggest a starting salary. Professors gave John an average score of 4 for competence and Jennifer a 3.3. The average starting salary offered to Jennifer was $26,508 while John's average was $30,328. Interestingly, the bias had no relation to the professor's age, gender, or tenure. Women professors had the same bias as male professors.

Everyone has work to do to be aware of implicit or unconscious bias. But it isn't the sole role of women, who are on the receiving end of the bias, to raise the issues. As men, we have a role in calling gender issues out with other men.

"What did your daughter do, Lee?" asked Joe.

"She moved to a smaller accounting firm that had a lot more women. She is a lot happier. So am I."

"Unfortunately, that is not an uncommon experience," said Bill. "It's still a male-dominated world in many companies, especially at the top. The latest surveys show that only 6.1 percent of Fortune 1000 company CEOs are female, 16.3 percent of Fortune 500 board directors are female, and 14.1 percent of executive officers are women."

I jumped in where Bill left off. "Yet those women have enormous value. When Credit Suisse examined 2,400 global corporations from 2005 to 2011, before and after the last financial crisis, they found that large-cap companies with at least one woman on their boards outperformed comparable companies with all-male boards by 26 percent."

"Why was that?" asked Frank. "Simply because they had a woman on their board?"

"I'm sure it's complex, but it sure is an interesting correlation," I answered. "There is research to suggest men take more risks when stressed, tied to larger spikes in the stress hormone cortisol. Stressed woman tend to make more advantageous decisions in these studies. Men are also less aware of their using more risky strategies when stressed. Perhaps that is why backcountry ski groups with a woman in the group are statistically less likely to be caught in avalanches. There is also evidence that under stressful conditions, women become more attuned to others. In that way, women can make groups smarter."

"Except that in our white male culture, which permeates most business organizations, women don't often feel like they can use their unique strengths such as intuition, emotional literacy, multitasking, or deeper collaboration," added Bill.

"Yes, the same research showing that women make a group smarter also showed that effect being lost when competition for status is introduced into the group. Competition and status are certainly part of our white male culture," I said.

I was aware we were presenting a lot of data for the men to absorb. It was a risky thing to do because it usually causes guys to go into their heads, an intellectual place without the heart connection. But I was amazed to see that was not happening tonight. The men were moved by the experience of Lee's daughter and were still reeling from Joe's disclosure about his terminally ill son.

"Hey, Frank," said Al, "remember our female colleague who was here on Monday before the caucus? The one I said you hardly looked at or addressed during our lunch?"

"Yes," Frank answered, somewhat sheepishly. "What about her?"

"She's probably experienced a lot of this stuff."

"It sounds like she experienced some of it with you, Frank," said Lee, "during our lunch."

Frank was startled. "Yes. I think I owe her an apology."

"Frank, you had an impact on her that you didn't intend," I said. "That creates an opportunity to go back and simply ask how you impacted her. It will likely deepen your partnerships with her. That will be much more useful than defending your intent and trying to prove you're a good guy."

Frank seemed to consider this. His face was less red.

"This actually addresses another radical thought habit for us," I said.

MINDSET #10

Be conscious of intent and impact. By tuning into both the intent and impact we have on each other, we build a foundation for full partnership.

In fact, anytime we bump into a person at work in some way and cause conflict, it becomes an opportunity to create a stronger partnership. Norms are not created by critical events. They are created by how we respond to those critical events. Circling back to have a conversation to learn about your impact and how it was not aligned with your intent opens up possibilities and creates shared understanding.

FIFTEEN

Exploring Male Privilege

THE ROCKING CHAIRS WERE MOVING BACK AND FORTH as we continued into the evening. The men showed fatigue from the work we'd been doing all week. Nevertheless they were all engaged. Frank seemed to still be pondering the challenge he had just received. Now it was time to revisit the concept of privilege, or systemic advantage, with a gender lens rather than a race lens.

"How many of you have had someone assume that you were the office assistant in your office environment or at business meetings you attend?" I asked.

No one raised his hand.

"This can be a common experience for women," I continued. "For men, having that experience is rare. You might recall your initial reactions to this concept of privilege when we earlier explored it."

"Honestly, I left that conversation still in denial," said Frank. "I hate the word 'privilege.' I went to my room and looked in the bathroom mirror and said, 'I'm not privileged.' Well, after a few more hours I went back to that mirror and said, 'I am privileged.' Though I'm not saying I like the word. I hate that word."

The men laughed, perhaps because they had also been uncomfortable with the idea of privilege.

"I found the concept of privilege helpful," said Lee. "Frank, it's not about us having everything handed to us or not working hard. It's about the stuff we don't have to manage or deal with. I realized not only are we fish in water, but we also have the current on our side. We still have to swim, but we can swim a lot faster."

"So, let's brainstorm examples of male privilege," said Bill. "Stuff we don't have to think about or deal with because we are male."

After a few minutes of quiet reflection, I shared a list of examples to further their thinking.

FOURTEEN EXAMPLES OF MALE PRIVILEGE

1. I can list my full name in the phone book or on the web and not receive harassing or obscene phone calls or emails.

2. If I am heterosexual, my sexual partner is expected to take more responsibility for birth control.

3. I am judged less for the attractiveness of my appearance.

4. I can walk the streets without being the object of gawks, whistles, catcalls, harassment, or attacks because of my gender.

5. I am not expected to be overly attentive or to wait on people.

6. I can walk into a car repair garage, hardware store, or electronics shop and usually expect someone to answer my questions without being condescending to me.

7. I am rarely if ever judged on the cleanliness or neatness of my house.

8. I don't worry about the threat of rape or sexual violence due to my gender. It is not an undercurrent that impedes my moving freely.

9. I can make mistakes, fail miserably on a project, or be fired from a job without anyone attributing it to my gender.

10. I am generally part of the gender majority in most higher-level workplace meetings I attend.

11. I can easily find mentors of my gender at all levels in the organization.

12. My ability to function effectively during crisis is not questioned because of my gender.

13. I do not experience being patronized because of my gender.

14. I enjoy company-sponsored social events and/or teambuilding that usually cater to what are considered male activities (hunting, golf, fishing, etc.).

After giving them a chance to consider our examples for a while, Bill asked what else they came up with.

Lee spoke first. "I don't have to find a spot to pump breast milk."

"I don't think I'd want your milk," joked Joe.

Lee did not laugh.

"Seriously," said Lee. "When my daughter had her first child there were no places for her to go. She had to go out to the parking lot and pump milk for her baby in the back seat of her car. Then she had to put the milk in a cooler she kept in the car."

"That sucks," admitted Joe.

Joe spoke next, "I don't have to expend time or energy to ensure my travel arrangements help me avoid the threat of rape or sexual violence."

The men stared at him as they seemed to reflect.

"It's true. I regularly arrive late at night into airports and don't worry about the location of my hotel room or where I have to go to get food," added Al.

"Well, that's wrong, I've had to worry about where I go at night," countered Frank.

"Yes, Frank, but notice how rarely that occurs for you versus many of your women colleagues," replied Bill.

Joe jumped back in. "The examples of having to monitor yourself constantly for safety just really strike me. I've heard of women who walk to their car at night with their keys between their knuckles in case someone jumps out at them."

"Here's another thing. I can put family events on my work calendar," said Lee. "I know a female leader who is afraid to put them on her calendar because others might conclude she can't balance work and family. Instead, I am seen as a dedicated dad."

Frank raised his hand.

"Frank?" I asked.

"I just realized something. I have been trying to hire a male assistant so that I don't have to worry about whether I will offend him."

"That sounds like some sort of privilege," said Al. "Being able to stick to the boys' club so you don't have to be so careful."

Frank swallowed hard.

"Thank you for calling that out, Frank," said Bill.

"But there are women who are very foulmouthed," claimed Frank. "If I say the same stuff, I am reported to HR." Frank shook his head.

"On the other hand, we worked with an executive team who called themselves the pirates," said Bill. "They were very foul mouthed in their hardcore bantering with each other. It turns out they were alienating most women around them, and they didn't even know it."

"What's important is that we as men learn to recognize these things and help each other see them," I said. "It's not okay to have women always be the ones to have to bring up these issues. They have their own jobs to do rather than spending their waking hours educating and reeducating us. And when they do bring it up, they are often seen as having a chip on their shoulders. Or what they're saying is doubted, and they're told to prove the problem is real."

I knew all too well how easy it was to be blind to these privileges and how my daily life in the world is different because I'm a man. Even when it's right in front of me.

I shared a story to illustrate this point. Once Bill and I were flying in from different locations to Kalamazoo, Michigan, to present to a senior executive team. Thunderstorms closed O'Hare airport for several hours. I was grounded in Cedar Rapids but eventually made it to O'Hare. Bill was grounded in Rockford, Illinois. He finally got off the plane with his bags and found a local taxi to take him to Chicago. Meanwhile, I found there were no more flights and no more rental cars to get to Kalamazoo.

Eventually Bill pulled up at the airport in this taxi that had the insulation falling out of the roof and a very skinny cab driver who looked ill. I hesitated half a second, but Bill had already arranged it, so I jumped in. Bill had offered the driver $400 to take us to Kalamazoo. And we had to buy him a map of Chicago so he could find his way home. He had never been out of Rockford. When we got to Kalamazoo at 2:30 a.m. and offered the cab driver a hotel room, his dispatch told him he had to drive back immediately because they needed the cab by 7:30 a.m. The man was afraid to say no because he was a single parent and didn't want to lose his job.

That gave us an unexpected insight into both class privilege and gender expectations, as he was forced to obey orders and continue with no sleep. As executive consultants, we were sleeping in cushy hotel rooms.

At our session the next day we proudly told the executive team of our adventure in the taxi. One woman on the team said, "I would never have ridden in a taxi across rural America through the night, and I would have made up an excuse rather than tell you I was afraid. I wouldn't want you to think I wasn't a team player."

Bill and I looked at each other. Until she spoke up, neither of us had recognized that this was another example of male privilege. And we teach this for a living. Sometimes it can be almost too close to see, which is why we need male colleagues to actively challenge us in continuous learning. The men sat in reflection.

"Any of you realize you were not seeing something like this right in front of you?" I asked.

Al scratched his goatee and spoke, "I was congratulating another guy in my office as I was giving him an employee award. I said I was impressed how hard he worked so that his wife could stay home. Boy, later I felt like an idiot thinking about how that felt for all the women in that room. Another guy mentioned something to me."

Joe straightened himself up in his chair. "Yeah. You guys know I like to think in black and white. I don't like ambiguity. If I get emotional I tell myself I'm not thinking clearly. Well, one time my wife was crying, and I was making lots of suggestions. She stopped me and asked, 'Have I given you any indication that I'm stupid or weak?' I said, 'No, but you're crying—I thought you needed some help.' She said, 'No, that's just my way of processing my experience.' I'm learning not to equate crying or emotion as weakness."

"Tears for some women can mean anger, too, so you can't assume it's sadness," I added.

"Also, it used to be if I saw my wife was crabby, I would say, 'I'll talk to you tomorrow,'" continued Joe. "I realized eventually I was moving away from rather than toward her, and I wasn't there for her while she expressed her emotions."

Frank was nodding and responded, "I do that, too. But does that make me sexist?"

Lee was brushing a cookie crumb off his shirt. "I used to think I was not sexist or racist because I was not taking active actions to foster prejudice. But now I am realizing racism and sexism are not solely defined by action but by lack of awareness of their systemic existence."

"Now this is interesting," said Bill. "We can be fighting sexism and in collusion with it at the same time. In fact, it's likely, given that we've been immersed in it our entire lives. We need to be on a long-term journey of awareness and action."

Sometimes taking action can have negative consequences. Across a series of studies, when men took action to promote women's rights, people responded with surprise and anger. Both men and women were shocked and resentful toward the men. Their motives were questioned. When intervening, there is also a risk of being kicked out of the boys' club. These challenges force us to develop the Leadership Skill of Managing Difficult Conversations. This includes the willingness to initiate tough conversations by leaning into them rather than away from them. One key is to start by clearly stating your intent and affirm the importance of the partnership. Other skills come into play here, such as courage, listening, and integrating head and heart. I have learned from the book *Difficult Conversations* to see each person's perspective as valid and to be watchful so that I don't attribute negative intent or character to others.

Bill told a story that showed how engaging in challenging conversations can result in rejection. "My brother once intervened with a bunch of golfing colleagues. One of the more senior leaders of the group sent out an email with an inappropriate gender joke. My brother ended up replying and saying he didn't want to receive those emails, and he advised his colleague not to send them. As a result, he was kicked out of the golf club and no longer invited to play golf with that group of guys. He realized, like many of us do, that relationships may end when you challenge other men on these topics."

I saw curiosity on the faces pointed toward Bill.

"Maybe he didn't want to play golf with those guys anyway," sympathized Al.

Bill added, "One of our African American colleagues, Cherie Buckner-Webb, likes to say, 'I don't want you to get rid of your privilege. I want you to use it honorably.' You can use your privilege to challenge male colleagues, whereas a woman saying the same thing might be seen as having a chip on her shoulder."

SIXTEEN

Objectifying Women

SNACK PLATES, COFFEE CUPS, AND SODA CANS WERE scattered on the floor by the rocking chairs—growing piles of remnants from our evening conversations thus far. We still had another hour in our Wednesday evening. It was time to address an aspect of gender often undiscussed: our objectification of women.

We watched twenty minutes of Jean Kilbourne's movie *Killing Us Softly 4: Advertising's Image of Women*. We'd been showing her movies, now updated four times, for twenty years. Men usually find it shocking how many images of women in the media are digitally altered. Then we turned the lights back up.

"Gentlemen, let's work off a few of those dinner and snack calories," said Bill jokingly. "Michael and I will be reading a series of statements, one statement at a time, and the invitation is to stand up silently if that statement applies to you and you choose to disclose that." Bill nodded at me.

I read the first statement, "Please stand if you have ever discussed a woman's body with other men."

All of the men stood up. Frank snickered.

"Thanks," I said as the others followed me in sitting back down.

Bill read the next statement. "Please stand if you have ever read or viewed sexually explicit literature or magazines or pornographic movies that objectified women as sex objects."

This time everyone in the room stood up but Lee.

"Should I just stay standing?" asked Frank.

The other men laughed.

"I'm with ya, Frank," said Al.

"Go ahead and sit," I said. "Getting up and down burns calories."

Everyone snickered this time.

I continued, "Please stand if you have been fixated on a particular part of a woman's anatomy—breasts, legs, buttocks, or whatever."

Again all the men stood up. A hush fell over the room as the men began to realize the extent of their objectification of women.

Bill continued, "Please stand if you have regularly fantasized about being sexual with a woman you noticed on the street or other public place and had never met before."

Everyone rose.

We followed with twenty-two other statements, each time with similar results. Then we invited the men to share what was on their minds.

"I'm even more scared for my daughters now," said Lee as he adjusted his glasses. "Our male culture really reinforces our seeing women as sexual objects."

"I think some of this is human nature," answered Joe. "I can't just shut off my sexual nature. It's pretty ingrained."

There are both hormones and cultural influences at stake. Joe wanted the hormonal side acknowledged. I remembered seeing an article on transgender people in the *New York Times*. They interviewed a person who had transitioned from woman to man and, as part of the process, was taking the same amount of testosterone as the average man has naturally. He was quoted as saying, "I felt like if I didn't have sex every day, I was going to die." That's a strong statement of the impact of testosterone. But we can't simply blame hormones for men's behavior. There are also strong cultural influences at play.

"All those magazines with the models photoshopped— those magazines are bought by women," said Al. "They are perpetuating those images by paying for them. If they want to change the situation, they shouldn't buy them."

I struggled briefly to try to get a sense of the best way to acknowledge Al's perspective and offer an additional perspective to bring the focus back to our role as men in this complex dynamic. Even after doing caucuses for twenty years, I can struggle to challenge my colleagues when they come up with what could be seen as blaming the victim, in this case women, for the objectification that they experience. I returned to the trusty adage: all perspectives are valid and likely incomplete.

"Okay, guys, first we blamed the hormones, then we blamed women. Let's look in the mirror to examine our part in objectifying women." I saw that Al seemed agitated.

"I was part of a fraternity in college," said Bill. "I am

embarrassed at the attitudes and behaviors we perpetuated. There were times when it felt like women were objects of conquest to win and to display like trophies of status."

"I experienced some of that culture too," I added. I was still gazing at Al.

Al leaned forward in his chair. "Okay, so sometimes when I am at work talking to a woman admin, or any woman for that matter, I mentally undress her." He paused. "I mean it's just for fun, it doesn't in anyway impact my relationships with them."

The men stopped rocking their chairs and stared at Al in shock. He sensed the pause and their eyes on him.

"It's just a thing I do in the back of my mind to entertain myself," said Al.

I was surprised myself, not expecting this from Al. I wondered who was going to say something and whether Al would be challenged. Frank's eyes were wide.

"That's bullshit," said Lee. "How can you say that doesn't affect your relationships with them? They are talking to you about work, and you are picturing them naked?"

"It doesn't," replied Al. "I'm telling you it doesn't."

"How can it not?" asked Lee. "I mean, really. I'm thinking about you doing that to my daughter. I want to kick your ass."

This was the first time Lee had appeared angry, and he had everyone's attention. Lee felt bigger in the room to me. Meanwhile Al was shrinking slightly in his chair. I feared he might revert back to his earlier self in the caucus, when he was shy and wanted the other guys' approval. It would be good for him to stick up for himself, I thought, while learning others' perspectives here.

"We all stood up for the statement that referred to thinking about being sexual with a woman on the street we didn't know," I said. "I don't believe Al is the only one here who has some version of objectification going on in his life."

I turned to Lee. "Lee, I appreciate your challenging other guys on their objectification of women. What do others think?"

Frank tightened his square jaw and addressed Al. "You challenged me for ignoring Joan at our lunch meeting Monday, Al. I have come to appreciate your feedback. So I have some feedback for you. Do you think it's possible that your mental undressing habit is impacting your partnerships with women in ways you don't know? For instance, is there a part of your brain that isn't fully present to them and what they are saying?"

Al shrugged his shoulders. "It's possible . . ."

Frank leaned forward and softened his voice. "Is it okay if I refer to our dinner conversation?"

Al nodded.

"You told me you have a daughter who hasn't spoken to you in two years," Frank continued. "Would you want a guy to mentally undress her at work?"

Al turned red and choked up. My eyes searched the room for water in case he needed some. I tossed the Kleenex box over by his feet as I noticed a tear form in the corner of his eye.

"Now I'm thinking about why my daughter doesn't talk

to me," Al said. "Maybe she felt my lack of presence." He ignored the Kleenex and wiped his eye with the back of his hand. "When she hit puberty and began to develop sexually I stopped hugging her and became more withdrawn. I was afraid of being attracted to her. I didn't want to be inappropriate." His voice trailed off and he took a deep breath.

I sat there grateful for the blunt advice one of my female colleagues gave me when she discovered I had two young daughters. She said, "Don't you be one of those dads who disappears when your daughters start looking like women because you're afraid of your own arousal. Don't let *your* discomfort get in the way of being a dad."

I turned to Al. "When you backed off from your daughter, whose discomfort were you taking care of—hers or yours?"

The question stopped Al in his tracks.

"Mine," he replied. Another tear fell.

"My daughter also struggled with anorexia," Al said.

I thought of my own daughter in her early teens. And the pressure women feel to fit images of beauty in the media. I remembered how she and her friends wished they were like the skinny girls and weren't happy with the way they looked. At the time I felt uncertainty about how well I was handling my own daughters' need to be acknowledged for their beauty and at the same time not giving it too much value. Would I someday feel regret like Al was experiencing now? I wanted to make sure I also reflected on how strong, how smart, and how courageous they are. When I read the book *Strong Fathers, Strong Daughters,* I was surprised at the number of studies showing the critical role a father plays on a daughter's healthy sense of herself. One study showed that the strongest predictor of a daughter's self-esteem was her father's physical affection.

Al sat there pondering the feedback he had received. Frank got up to get a soda and squeezed Al's shoulder as he walked by. Clearly, the men in the room cared about Al, who had always brought a heartfelt presence into the room. Now he was the recipient of heartfelt gestures from other men.

Joe spoke up. "My wife had jaw surgery a few years ago. She was never happy with the way her jaw looked. I never understood why she wanted to change her body. This conversation helps me understand the pressure she must have felt to look like some ideal. I can imagine where she was coming from." A shadow fell across Joe's face. "Something went wrong in the surgery," he said sadly. "Now she doesn't like to go out in public. She stays home a lot." He stared at the floor with a big sigh. "I don't know how to help her feel better about herself. She has withdrawn and is slowly losing some of her longtime friends."

The room was silent as Joe shared this painful experience for him and his wife. The pressure women feel regarding their appearance is a foreign idea for most men, yet it impacts girls and women all around us.

Lee addressed Joe. "I wouldn't know what to do in that situation, Joe, but I am glad you are there to support her."

"We can't always protect the women in our lives," Lee said. "My daughter was assaulted a few years ago in a New York City subway. A man came up behind her and grabbed her."

He shook his head and continued, "I asked her why she didn't shout for help. She said, "Well, he could have had a knife.""

"So then what happened?" asked Joe.

"Fortunately a man got between her and the assailant," said Lee.

"This is much more common than many of us think," said Bill. "According to research from the United Nations, 35 percent of women worldwide have experienced either physical and/or sexual intimate-partner violence or non-partner sexual violence. In the United States, nearly one in five women are raped. You and I don't walk around with a 20 percent chance of being raped."

I was ready to add more, but I paused to let the group digest that astounding statistic. I saw some of the men's eyes widen.

"If you take it into the workplace, recent studies show *one in four* women have experienced workplace sexual harassment," I added. "As a man, I don't walk around the workplace with a 25 percent chance of experiencing sexual harassment."

Bill leaned toward Lee. "I'm sorry that happened to your daughter," he said. "Every woman is someone's daughter. It's our job as men to break up the collusion among men that has us allowing this harassment to continue, especially in the workplace."

Frank was getting upset. "Al, that's why your mentally undressing women at work bothers me," he said. "It contributes to connecting to women more as objects than as human beings."

Frank scanned the whole group. "If we are talking at work as a group of men and we have to stop the conversation when a woman walks into the room, perhaps it's not a conversation we should be having in the first place."

Joe spoke up next. "I was once in a police shift meeting a few years back," he said. "It was the beginning of a new shift, and we were getting briefed on current status before going out on patrol. One man announced to the room he had a young woman riding with him from the community that day. Another guy called out to him, 'Is she hot?' There were woman cops in the room who had to put up with that stuff."

"Did you say anything?" asked Lee.

"Honestly, I found myself starting to laugh along with the rest of the room, as I've been dealing with this throughout my career. Then I realized that wasn't okay, and I went and told the guy afterward. I also went back to the women cops and asked them what it was like to hear that."

"What did they say?" asked Lee.

"They brushed it off," replied Joe. "But they'd been there for twenty years—they had to ignore it to survive. The conversation with the guy was harder. He accused me of being the 'PC police.'"

Indeed, I knew the biggest challenge was for men to confront other men about these issues, and to do it without looking to women for their approval. We have to be willing to put our relationships with other men at risk as we break up our own collusion around treating women as something less than human beings at work.

Intervening with other white men requires the Leadership Skill of Courage. Courage includes standing by your principles and taking a risk in spite of fear. Sometimes courage looks like saying "I don't know" or sharing vulnerably your learning journey and blind spots. This gives others permission to show their human side as well.

It had been a long full day and was time for rest. Naming courage was a good place to pause for the night.

SEVENTEEN

Our Avoidance and Hunger for Nurturance

THURSDAY, THE SKIES WERE CLEAR AS WE WATCHED Snappy eat Frank's breakfast sausage. Frank seemed to have a growing connection with the 300-pound alligator snapping turtle, who had become our mascot. We discovered partway through the week that alligator snapping turtles are carnivores. It always impressed me how clear animals are about what they need and want. In the three days we'd spent together, this group of men was just beginning to find out.

As we walked from breakfast to the meeting room, Bill and I had to make a choice about whether to start with a provocative activity for the morning. It was an activity we were reluctant to use with corporate audiences after one attempt, when many of the men refused to participate. We felt this group was ready for it.

After kicking off the day and hearing a few overnight reflections from the guys, I glanced at Bill and gave him a nod.

"We have something new for you," said Bill. "It's an exercise where you will pair up with another man."

A couple of the men began to grumble.

Bill persisted. "Go sit next to someone you want to work with."

The men in the room moved around. Frank and Al sat together, and Lee and Joe scooted their chairs together. They watched Bill in anticipation. I felt my heart beat faster as I knew this would be a stretch for the guys.

"Okay, great," said Bill. "In this exercise you may bump up against your gender role conditioning as men. Remember this is an exercise in this retreat, I'm not asking you to do this at work."

I saw Frank's eyes grow big. Most of the men in fact seemed startled.

"I want you to spend ten minutes nurturing your partner without talking," Bill said. "You need to ask the other what they want first."

Everyone looked puzzled.

I stood up. "Here is one example." I walked over to behind Bill's chair and massaged his shoulders for ten seconds. Bill let out a sigh.

Some of the men chuckled.

"This may be a stretch for some of you, but you can do this," I said.

I sat down on the floor in front of Bill's chair. He got out of his chair and sat in my lap and I held him, gently swaying. Again I felt him let out a sigh of relaxation. I remembered a caucus years earlier when he actually sobbed in my arms.

A few of the men burst out laughing.

"Okay, it may seem silly, but negotiate whatever level of nurturance you are comfortable with and try that and notice whatever comes up for you," said Bill. "If you need to stop and change something, you can. Renegotiate in the moment. Step out of your comfort zone to a learning zone but not to a danger zone."

At once the men began talking. Words were flying between the pairs. The first time we tried this years ago in a corporate group, several men had jumped to their feet and scooted toward the door within ten seconds, announcing they would take a walk together as a form of nurturance. My anxiety was surging. But this time the men stayed.

I saw that Frank and Al were in an intense conversation. They had defaulted to talking their way through the exercise time.

"Only one more minute of talking before doing the nonverbal exercise," I shouted.

Lee was already sitting on the floor in front of Joe's chair as Joe gave him a shoulder massage. Joe had clearly appreciated Lee helping him talk to the TV reporter the previous day. Lee's head fell down against his chest as he let go.

Bill was still sitting in my lap.

"What do you want, Bill?" I asked.

"Just hold me," replied Bill.

Bill weighed slightly more than me, but as I sat there on the floor, I leaned my back against a chair for support. Having been business partners for twenty years, I felt my comfort and satisfaction in holding a good friend. I also noticed a wave of discomfort, wondering how other men might feel seeing us being more intimate than most men. I wondered what the hospitality staff would think if they wandered into the room. I felt Bill sink into me as he relaxed. We were naturally breathing in sync. I felt the background of the room fade away as I simply felt myself being present with Bill.

It was quite a bit later when, glancing around the room, I was surprised to see Al sitting on the floor leaning into Frank who was also sitting on the floor with the wall right behind him. Wow. They were really willing to try some nurturing. This pleased me, knowing they both deserved more support.

Fifteen minutes later we were gathered back in our circle. I saw both tense faces and relaxed faces.

"So what was that like?" asked Bill.

"Scary as hell," answered Al. "I can't believe you asked us to do that. I almost walked out."

A laugh erupted across the room.

"What was so scary about it, Al?" I asked.

"I don't know. There was just this terror," said Al.

"Terror of . . ."

"Like I was remembering all the times when I was called names."

"What names?" I asked.

"Fag, homo, mama's boy."

"Afraid of being seen as gay," said Lee. "I lived that my whole childhood. Once I was held down on the playground. Guys peed in my mouth because they thought I was gay."

The room paused as the guys took in this horrific story.

"That was me," said Joe. "I was one of those guys. On another playground in another city, across the country. Some guys and I held a guy down and we peed in his mouth, and I'm sorry."

Joe was leaning across the circle toward Lee with a heart-felt tone of apology.

No one in the room spoke for a minute.

Lee had tears welling up in his eyes as he turned to Joe and took in his heartfelt apology, an apology he never expected or even dreamed possible. An apology Joe never thought he could give. There had been many serendipitous moments like this across twenty years of caucuses. This was one I would never forget.

"Lee, what's it like to hear Joe say that?" I asked.

Lee wiped a tear from his eye. "It feels good," Lee said. "And thanks for the shoulder rub Joe—that was great, too. I didn't realize how I never receive supportive touch from another guy unless it's just some kind of high five."

As I sat there I suddenly had a memory of my father putting suntan lotion on my back when I was a child. It was always so special feeling his strong hands gently touching me. Our homophobic male culture robs us of that touch and nurturance.

"Even at a family wedding, my dad would only shake hands with me," said Frank. "Then my father-in-law walked over and hugged me. It felt awkward. I've never told my dad I love him."

The father-son connection was a great example of how we learn to be distant from each other as men. We learn to be stoic and never show vulnerability, and are often starved for nurturance.

Lee spoke up. "I called my dad yesterday on the break, and I told him what I was learning here about privilege. I told him I appreciate how much he and Mom worked so hard so I could benefit."

"What did he say?" asked Frank.

"There was this long pause and then he just said, 'I'm glad you're having a good session,'" Lee said. "He didn't acknowledge the appreciation."

"I had the same kind of response from my dad," said Joe. At the end of one of my calls last month, I said a quick 'I love you.' He asked, 'What did you say?' I told him again, and he just said 'Oh.'"

Sitting there listening to the conversation reminded me of when I told my dad I loved him for the first time. I was twenty-one years old. He said, "Well you've been a good son, so far." I had just switched my major from electrical engineering to psychology, and he was afraid I was going to join some commune. Telling him I loved him probably made him even more worried. It was one of those times when I learned to go ahead and do something because it was what I needed and not try to figure out what he wanted. I laughed to myself. I guess I was becoming more like Snappy, going for what I wanted and needed. Maybe it would even help me live longer like him!

I saw Al scratching his goatee. I could tell he wanted to speak.

"I've noticed when there are only white men in the room at work I can't reveal myself as much. I'm more courageous when women and people of color are in the room," said Al. "It's something about my image and what they think of me. I can't share with the guys as much."

"I told you," started Frank. "I think you need to get over your need for approval."

"So you think you are more afraid of white guys judging you?" I asked.

"I guess so," said Al.

"You're supposed to belong to the white male club, so to speak," said Bill. "But within our group there is a strong sense of status and rank. We can be pretty tough, especially if we perceive someone as touchy-feely or too soft."

"Exactly," said Joe. "I thought it was my job to toughen up my next older brother. So I was rough with him. He came out to me last."

"As gay?" I asked.

"Yes," said Joe. "I guess he felt I was the least safe to tell."

Bill then shared a story of a time when we did a caucus for a power company. It was all linemen who strung up the power lines and went out to repair them. There was a guy who came out to both of us facilitators but not to the group. He was certain he'd be harassed.

Lee spoke, "During high school, my cousin was part of a group that beat the crap out of a guy. They thought he was gay. I fought it. I told them they can't do that. As a result, I was ostracized for the rest of high school. Three weeks later that guy committed suicide."

"You were courageous for speaking out, Lee," said Bill.

"It sounds like it cost you friendships. That can happen when we challenge norms that are unhealthy. Sometimes we make new friends that are more meaningful."

"Yeah," said Lee. "I lost friends. I made a few new ones, but I was often lonely."

I jumped in. "Lee, your story reminds me of the Leadership Skill of Being an Agent of Change. It's the opportunity to apply all the other leadership skills to create the kind of world you want to live in. As Gandhi said, 'You must be the change you want to see in the world.' I am moved by how you challenged the status quo among your peers."

"Sometimes you are the lone voice," said Bill. "If you don't speak up, sometimes you regret that, too. There was a woman in a session who told of how her son came out as gay. Her husband kicked him out and banned him from the family. It was really tough for her. Then her son was killed in a motorcycle accident. Now she regrets every day not finding a way to challenge her husband and stay connected to her son."

One must become an agent of change in order to lead. This is not always comfortable and requires the courage to challenge others.

EIGHTEEN

The Collision of Sexual Orientation and Religion

THE RISKY NURTURANCE EXERCISE HAD PUSHED against the homophobia many men possess. Regardless of our sexual orientation, virtually all white men have been raised in an environment where homophobia is woven into our gender conditioning. As I looked around the group, I could tell some of the men were still reeling from the extreme edginess of the nurturing exercise. While it is powerful for some, it is too much of a stretch for others. Now trying it after a long hiatus (we hadn't done it in eighteen years), Bill and I recognized it was still too edgy for a corporate audience. I guess everyone does wild things in their early days that they don't do today, and that's true for our company as well. There is still plenty of material we cover in the White Men's Caucus that is way outside the norm of the corporate business world. We, in fact, pride ourselves in stepping outside the habits of corporate white men in order to create lasting, heartful insights.

We had just viewed part of a film by Brian McNaught

called *Homophobia in the Workplace*, and it was time to open up the group for conversation.

"Let's expand from our focus on homophobia as it relates to gender conditioning in men to the topic of sexual orientation," I said. "There are two things to note as we begin this conversation. First, we don't presume to know that we are all a group of heterosexual men. Second, this is not meant as an attempt to change your religious beliefs. There is actually room for you to hold onto whatever beliefs you already have and still have empathy for others who are different and support their right to be who they are in the workplace. People don't need to agree on all kinds of moral issues in order to work together."

I expected my religious comment might resonate with somebody in the group.

Frank suddenly let out a storm of frustration. "Look, I don't know how I can support gays. It's against my religious beliefs. I'm tired of having this issue shoved down my throat. I do feel like I am being asked to change my religious beliefs. They're a core part of who I am, but I can't even have a Bible on my desk or a poster honoring my religion on my wall. I am told it offends people. Yet people go around flaunting their sexual orientation. Their email signatures advertise gay pride month, as do the posters on their walls."

Frank let out a huge sigh. The room was silent for a few seconds. I struggled with how to support Frank while also creating space for those he may have just offended. Often sexual orientation and religious values are assumed to be in opposition; it's assumed they can't coexist.

Bill jumped in. "I really appreciate you putting your voice out there, Frank," he said. "It's gotta be tough not to be able to bring such a core part of you to work."

"Absolutely," replied Frank. "I can't even say Merry Christmas. I read an editorial from a CEO supporting gay marriage. He called it a moral imperative. How come he gets to take a moral stand, and I get called to task for speaking my morals?"

Bill and I had seen this type of reaction many times over the years. We had worked with another organization that had routinely started their meetings with prayer. They'd only recently stopped doing that, and it was a hard change for some of their leaders. They'd realized they had a right to believe whatever they believe, but they didn't have a right to impose that belief on others.

Frank looked upset. "Some of these gays are pretty promiscuous, on top of everything else!" he blurted out.

Joe was shaking his head vehemently. "Wait a minute. Sure, there are promiscuous people out there, whether they're gay or straight. But one outrageous heterosexual at a Mardi Gras parade with a whip and chain doesn't mean all straight people are into S&M," he said.

"That's a good point," added Lee.

"I'm thinking about my gay brother," said Joe. "He isn't pushing some agenda at work. He is just struggling to be himself at work. He spent years hiding who he was. It cost him. Once he was up for a performance award, a paid vacation to Hawaii. All the past recipients had taken their spouses. But he didn't want to have to choose whether to go alone or come out and take his partner. So he actually underperformed at work so he wouldn't win the award."

"That's crazy," said Frank.

"It takes energy to hide part of yourself," said Bill. "Once a group of heterosexual executives were challenged to hide all evidence of their heterosexuality. They combed through their offices to remove pictures and censored what they said in conversation about their weekend activities. After a day of this, they were exhausted. It's hard not to bring your sexual orientation to work."

In fact, we flaunt our heterosexuality all the time.

"Heterosexuals are never viewed as flaunting their sexuality because it's considered normal," I said. "However, when homosexual or bisexual colleagues share who they are, it can be viewed as flaunting when actually they just want to be free to be themselves like we are every day."

Frank seemed to be pondering this.

"Look, I want people to be able to feel safe to be who they are," he said. "But when it comes to my family, I have a responsibility to teach them the religious values I hold."

"So what if your son was gay, Frank?" asked Lee.

"Well, my church says he would go to hell," replied Frank.

"Would you still love him?" said Lee.

Frank stared back, not knowing what to say. He appeared confused.

"Joe," I asked. "Did your brother tell your dad he was gay?"

"My dad had the same attitude as Frank, so my brother waited to come out until after our dad died," said Joe.

Frank's face was now white like his hair. Frank and Joe stared at each other.

"This issue can tear families apart," said Bill.

I reflected on my own evolution in understanding sexual orientation. My best friend from childhood came out to me after college. Later I learned several of my other close childhood friends were also gay. I had been surrounded by gay friends growing up in Iowa but didn't know it.

Some years later, I dated a woman who identified herself as bisexual. To honor her sexual orientation, we attended a predominantly gay and lesbian church in Minneapolis. I always wore one of the buttons they passed out at the entrance that said "straight but not narrow." Eventually I realized I was scared to death of others perceiving me as gay. Working through that internalized homophobia that most of us grew up with freed me to accept both my masculine and feminine aspects, regardless of how others perceived me.

Eventually I became able to be a better ally for others. One day after moving to Idaho, I was riding up the local ski chairlift with my fourteen-year-old nephew, who was living with us at the time. I turned to him and said out of the blue, "Micah, I don't know your sexual orientation, but I want you to know if you are gay, I love you." For some time I had wondered if he was. He choked up and couldn't talk for several minutes. It was the longest chairlift ride of my life. I figured I had just stressed him into needing therapy someday. I was relieved a few days later when he came up to me and thanked me for what I said. I still didn't know if he was gay, but I felt better about extending my love and acceptance. He came out a few years later to his family and friends. I am always inspired by his courage to be himself and speak his mind.

Then, about eight years ago, my twin sister came out as lesbian. It was our birthday, and afterward I talked to my dad on the phone. She'd told him a few weeks earlier. I asked my dad about it and he said, "Well I guess we'll tolerate that."

I said, "Dad, do you really mean *tolerate?* Do you still love her?"

"Yes, of course," he said.

I encouraged him to call her and tell her so. It was the first homosexual person my dad knew, his own daughter, and I felt good about being an ally to him much as others had been to me as I came to understand the complexity of sexual orientation.

I noticed that Frank, while still very reflective, had some color back in his face. I nodded at Bill for him to proceed.

"Let's dig at this a little deeper," Bill said. "The often unexamined aspect of sexual orientation is what it's like to be heterosexual. Let's explore what it means to be heterosexual through the lens of privilege. Take a few minutes to individually write in your journal pages and capture some examples of the heterosexual privileges many of us have. What are the things we don't have to navigate or deal with?"

I shared some examples.

TWELVE EXAMPLES OF HETEROSEXUAL PRIVILEGE

1. People don't ask why I made a choice to be public about my sexual orientation.

2. I don't have to routinely worry about the fear of discovery regarding my sexuality.

3. I will not be denied access to my partner's hospital bedside if there is a life-threatening illness or accident.

4. I openly dated the person of my choice when I was a teenager.

5. I did not grow up with games that attacked my sexual orientation (e.g., "fag tag" or "smear the queer").

6. I can freely talk about what I did over the weekend or on vacation without hiding or denying my family arrangement.

7. I can have a picture of my life partner on my desk at work without the risk of it negatively affecting my career or relationships with co-workers.

8. I don't have to agonize or worry about how to explain my sexual orientation to my children or their teachers.

9. I can expect to receive cards, phone calls, or Facebook congratulations in celebration of my commitment and/or marriage to another person.

10. My children don't have to worry about which of

their friends might reject them because of my sexual orientation.

11. I can expect paid leave from work and/or condolences when grieving the death of my partner/lover/spouse.

12. I don't have to feel the hurt or fear rejection from my parents, family of origin, or friends because of my sexual orientation.

"What examples did you all come up with?" asked Bill.

Frank leaned into the circle. "I can bring my partner home without fear of rejection from family members," he said.

"I don't have to worry about being fired or demoted from my job based on my sexual orientation," said Lee.

"Isn't that illegal?" asked Joe, surprised.

"It's still legal to do that in a majority of states," said Lee.

"I can bring my partner to company functions and offsite events to which spouses and significant others are invited, without the risk of it negatively affecting my career," said Al.

The men were nodding quietly.

"Here is another one," said Frank. "I often unknowingly assume people are heterosexual until I find out otherwise."

Joe looked at Frank thoughtfully. "I did that until my brother came out," he said.

"I don't have to worry about being 'saved,' 'fixed,' or 'healed' because of my sexual orientation," said Joe.

"Or attacked," added Lee.

"All this sounds exhausting," said Al. "If I had to deal with all this on top of the rest of my life, I would barely be able to function. Talk about a drain on my work productivity."

"I think I've made it harder than I realized for gay, lesbian, and bisexual people to be around me," said Frank. "By assuming they are imposing their beliefs on me I have felt threatened and haven't given them the space to simply be who they are."

"The root of the word 'impose' is *pose,* which comes from *ponere,* which means to place, put, or force upon," I said. "But most gay people are not trying to force or put anything on you—they are just trying to be themselves."

"You can hold whatever religious values you choose, Frank," said Bill. "And still be an ally. This is not an either/or; it's a both/and. People disagree all the time on moral issues such as abortion, capital punishment, and divorce, and yet we still work together. Sometimes it may take dialogue, but we can find space to coexist without imposing our beliefs on each other."

Frank's demeanor seemed momentarily lighter.

NINETEEN

Exploring Gender Identity and Generational Differences

WE WERE ABOUT TO GO INTO YET ANOTHER FRIGHT-
ening frontier for many white men. As the group was beginning to empathize with those who did not share their sexual
orientation, I saw confusion on Frank's face.

"I am starting to understand sexual orientation, but I'm
still really caught off guard with people changing their gender. An employee recently shared with me that they were
going through that transition, and I simply didn't know
what to say or do."

Frank was bringing us into the arena of gender identity.
This subject is fairly alien to many white men, including me.
Gender identity refers to the gender that a person claims
for oneself, which may or may not align with the gender
assigned at birth. *Cisgender* is a term that means you identify
with the gender you were assigned at birth. If you are *transgender*, you don't identify with the gender you were assigned
at birth. The white male cultural trait of low tolerance for
uncertainty reinforces thinking in either/or terms, which

means you can't conceive of anything but a dual world where a man is a man and a woman is a woman. But the human condition apparently is more complex. In fact, some people are actually born with body parts from both genders and/or see themselves somewhere on a gender continuum. Or they may be *gender fluid*, sometimes identifying themselves as a man and other times, as a woman. Others identify as *gender nonconforming*, where they don't want to participate with anything on a male-to-female gender spectrum.

Joe leaned forward. "Frank, when that person told you they were transitioning between genders, what did you say?"

"I didn't say much," confessed Frank.

"Have you seen this play out at work, Joe?" asked Al.

Seeing Joe nod yes, Al asked, "What happened?"

"There was a huge hoopla over which bathroom the transitioning employee would use," said Joe. "It was a man who was transitioning to a woman. Nobody wanted him—or her now—in their bathroom."

"What did you do then?" asked Al.

"We created a gender-neutral bathroom," said Joe. "She uses that bathroom. But before we built that bathroom, she had to go to one in another building about 100 yards away."

"I would hate having to do that," replied Frank.

"That's not all that wouldn't be easy," I said. "I recently read on the website of a nonprofit organization known as the Human Rights Campaign that 26 percent of transgender workers reported losing their job because of their gender identity, and 97 percent reported other negative experiences in the workplace—from verbal harassment to assault. If you do get to keep your job, think about how productive you can be at work while dealing with the harassment."

"We also talked to employees, let them ask questions, and told them we expected everyone to treat her respectfully," said Joe. "People asked useful questions like 'Which pronoun should I use?' But it's not okay for people to ask probing questions like what genitals they have."

"Look, guys," began Lee. "I actually have a younger niece who is really struggling with this."

The guys stopped, and all eyes were on Lee. It was unusual to hear heaviness in his voice.

Lee continued. "I've always been fairly close to her, and she shares with me openly. For the past couple years she has been withdrawing from her girlfriends and telling me she doesn't feel like them. She feels like she was meant to be a boy. She actually talked about suicide at one point." Lee's voice quaked, and his hand was shaking. "It tears me apart to see her struggle. For a while I didn't know what to do. I'm still getting used to the idea of calling her a *him*."

Lee's eyes were now filled with tears. "I am so moved by how her older sister has accepted this. And her two close boy cousins. They take her out every Wednesday on their boys' night out. It's so amazing—their acceptance. I am proud of their family as well as my soon-to-be nephew."

Frank's jaw was hanging open as he stared at Lee. Seeing this, Joe reached over and slapped Frank playfully on the shoulder, and Frank closed his mouth. Ironically, Joe was the one who typically didn't like ambiguity, but he seemed to be accepting the complexity of gender identity just fine.

Al leaned toward Lee and spoke softly from his heart. "Lee, I know you didn't have much of a father yourself. But all I can say is you are one hell of a good uncle and I imagine an amazing father."

I don't know that there was a dry eye left in the room. Everyone fell silent for a while, soaking in the tender moment.

After a few minutes Bill put on his reading glasses and picked up a paper by his chair. He read to the group examples he had just found on the Internet of cisgender privilege—things people who identify with the gender they were assigned at birth don't have to think about or navigate.

EXAMPLES OF CISGENDER PRIVILEGE

1. I can use facilities such as gym locker rooms and changing rooms in stores without stares, fear, or anxiety.

2. I have the ability to walk through the world and generally blend in, not being constantly stared or gawked at, whispered about, pointed at, or laughed at because of my gender expression.

3. I can purchase clothes that match my gender identity without being refused service/mocked by staff or questioned on my genitals.

4. Strangers checking my identification or driver's license will never insult or glare at me because my name or sex does not match the sex they believe I am based on my gender expression.

5. I am able to go to places with friends on a whim, knowing there will be bathrooms there I can use.

6. I don't have to remind my extended family over and over again to use proper gender pronouns (e.g., after transitioning).

7. I don't have to deal with old photographs that do not reflect who I truly am.

8. I don't have to worry about being placed in a sex-segregated detention center, holding facility, jail, or prison that is incongruent with my identity.

The men sat quietly listening.

"Here's another one," said Lee. "I can without difficulty or anxiety check gender boxes on forms that assume a permanent gender."

"I'm glad your other niece and nephews are so accepting, Lee," said Joe. "It seems to me like the younger generation is really more accepting of this stuff."

That was, in fact, true. One sign of that is that transgender people are coming out at younger and younger ages. According to research reports, in 2014, 69 percent of millennials favored same-sex marriage, compared to 37 percent of the generation sixty-eight years or older. That's a 32-point gap. But plenty of millennial youth who are gay, lesbian, bisexual, or transgender still face bullying and harassment, and they have elevated suicide rates. A 2013 study found 85 percent of LGBT young people reported experiencing verbal or physical harassment because of their sexual orientation or gender identity. An astounding 41 percent of transgender people have self-reported an attempted suicide, compared to 4.6 percent of the overall U.S. population. The numbers are elevated even more for transgender people who are minorities.

"The younger generation is something I wish we had talked about more here," said Frank. "I don't think I know how to partner with my younger employees."

"So let's talk about generational differences now," I said. "What do you most want to talk about, Frank?"

"Well, first of all, my kids don't get this focus we have on race," said Frank. "My son has friends of all colors. I asked him to describe one of his new friends to me when we were looking for him at the mall. Turns out he didn't even mention that he was black."

"My kids are the same way," said Al. "Maybe the race challenges will die with us."

"I wish that was the case," I said. "One of our clients did a White Men's Caucus just for their young employees. Most were in their late twenties and early thirties. They wanted to see if this stuff we've been discussing resonated with younger white male employees. Well, the younger guys found they had the same blind spots. Even though some of them may have had more friends of color, they had never thought about their white privilege and the things those friends had to negotiate and deal with daily. It was as eye opening for them as it was for us older white guys. There was one more interesting finding: being younger, they felt they weren't heard by their bosses and wondered whether to attribute it to their age. This experience made them empathize with the similar experiences of women and people of color."

I shared with them a 2014 study of millennials and bias conducted by MTV. In it, 84 percent of millennials said their families taught them everyone should be treated the same, no matter their race. And 89 percent actually do believe that everyone should be treated the same, no matter their race. But only 30 percent of white millennials were brought up in families that talked in detail about race. So differences are often not explored or discussed. In a 2012 MTV poll, 60 percent of white millennials believed discrimination affects white people just as much as it does people of color. In reaction to the statement "White people have more opportunity today than racial minority groups," 65 percent of youth of color will agree, whereas only 39 percent of white millennials do. Clearly there are different experiences and perceptions, but they are not being discussed across millennial color lines. They do want openness, as 73 percent of millennials believe we should talk more openly about bias. However, 79 percent worry about creating a conflict or making the situation worse.

"Thus, millennials have the same interest and need for dialogue skills as the older white men sitting around this circle," I concluded, noticing all the men were very interested in this conversation about age.

"That's fascinating," said Al. "It's true I never initiated discussions about race with my kids growing up. I just told them to treat everyone the same."

"Yes, so they have the same positive intent and the same blind spots that we do," I said.

For many whites, dialogues across race are unlikely to happen. According to a recent poll, 75 percent of white Americans have entirely white social networks.

I sensed there was more the guys wanted to share about their experience crossing generations.

"I just feel disrespected by the younger generation," said Al. "I once had a millennial woman who arrived ten minutes late for an interview. She wore jeans and took a cell phone call during the interview. As she took the call, she put her index finger up to me and gestured for me to wait a minute."

The guys laughed.

"I had a kid say 'Tell me why I should have this job,'" said Frank.

"Then there are the helicopter parents," said Al. I once rated an employee low, and I got a call from his mother. Another mom showed up with her kid at an interview."

"We are those parents, though," said Lee.

Bill added, "There was a *Fortune* magazine article a while back called 'You Raised Them, Now You Manage Them.'"

The guys laughed.

"It's true," said Lee. "And we sometimes just want to defend our way of doing things. Some of my customer service centers seem totally dysfunctional to me. The young folks are on Facebook, instant-messaging, playing music. But when I look at the numbers, they are my most productive group. So I focus on the deliverable and let them do it their way. Maybe they want to come in at 1 p.m. and work till midnight."

"Yes, we are also learning to think outside the box," added Frank. "Like adding pay scales so they get a promotion every six to nine months."

"It's important to sit down and get to know them as individuals," added Al. "Offer flexibility in scheduling, $100 iTunes cards, social events, and an informal dress code."

"Many millennials grew up watching their parents get laid off," I said. "They learned to be loyal to their career rather than loyal to one company. One large bank has accepted that and figured out how to leverage it. They created a formal alumni network and give everyone user names and passwords. They tell them they can always come back to the company. They reach out and support them doing social things as alumni. If today's youth are highly mobile, giving them a path to stay connected and come back to your organization is good business."

"That's a good idea," said Lee. "My company is big enough that we encourage employees to move around without having to leave the family."

"Perhaps our biggest obstacle is ourselves," said Bill. "What judgments and assumptions do you hold toward younger generations that get in the way of partnering?"

"I sometimes think they are lazy and want a promotion tomorrow," said Frank. "They don't seem to have the same hard work ethic."

"If you want lots of workers in tomorrow's world, you may need to offer better work–life balance than the workaholic mode you're used to," I said. "You put in your time over the years, and now you want them to play by the same rules. But notice, Frank, that your son didn't want anything to do with your company based on your 'never being around,' as he told you."

Frank's face showed a flash of pain.

"Partnering with millennials is a great place for you to practice all these leadership skills and radical habits," said Bill. "Get truly into inquiry and understand their world rather than judging them from your worldview."

"I also want to coach them to succeed," said Al. "I have coached younger folks to get out and touch flesh. Stop hiding behind technology. Get out among people and develop relationships."

I was glad Frank called for more time on exploring generational differences. The caucus format allowed for plenty of conversation on topics that were important and unique to the guys in the room. It was time to wind down this caucus and help the men identify key take-aways—action steps to begin to apply their learning, and complete their learning process with each other.

TWENTY

Seeing the Benefits

AFTER TWENTY-FIVE MINUTES OF BREAK WE RECON-vened for the last few hours in our caucus. Some of the men had put their luggage in their cars. While they were packed up physically, we still had important work to do to integrate our learning. We would now have them create some action plans to apply their learning back at work and home.

"This is an exclusive gathering of white men," said Bill. "Historically, white men don't have a positive track record when it comes to exclusive gatherings."

The men chuckled.

"So we invite you to take a few minutes to write out a few sentences of personal reflections directed to white women and people of color about the meaning of this caucus to you. Also write out a few other sentences directed to other white men. This will help you start to summarize your learning. Please turn them in when you're done."

I read the responses the men wrote to white women and people of color:

I am *sorry* that I have not fully understood the water that you swim in, the challenges that you deal with, and the things that I take for granted. I am committed to keeping these things in mind and changing or influencing for good where I am able.

—Frank

I would like to think I was open and aware of the issues surrounding diversity. After attending the workshop for four days, I saw how limited my perspective was. I'm just starting to understand what it means to belong to a white male group (which I didn't believe existed—but it does) and be an individual at the same time. My commitment is to continue to learn, grow, and be aware of differences in people so I can be open and work with them to make this a better place to be.

—Lee

Until now, I have never had to think about what it means to be a white male. I have learned that it comes with many privileges that I enjoy, but my privilege also has an impact on women and people of color. With this knowledge of myself, I feel I am better equipped to eliminate the oppression that occurs in the work environment and my personal life. However, I still feel confused in many areas and feel I'm at the beginning of a long journey.

—Al

First let me apologize for any impacts that I have unintentionally foisted on you. The White Men's Caucus has taught me several things—I unintentionally shut you off by trying to fix your issues instead of listening to your issues. I do not think from your viewpoint and your experience. I will change both of these behaviors to the best of my ability, but I need your help and patience as I evolve. Thank you.

—Joe

Next I read the responses the men wrote to other white men:

I appreciate the honest engagement from this entire group of white men—I have seen more courage in the last three days of this caucus than in my many years in my company. I will try to learn from what I witnessed.

—Lee

We cannot see what we may not understand or wish to understand. My truth is to understand others who are not white men and to take the journey with you as white men to a place where we may use our privilege as change agents.

—Joe

I had no concept of what other groups go through on a daily basis. We need to understand before we can solve problems, and as a white, male-dominated culture, we race to solve problems when the race should be to understand.

—Frank

Over ten years ago I began the diversity journey, full of energy and wanting to do what's right. Along the way I learned to become resentful and angry about the process and progress of women, people of color, and gay/lesbian groups. It felt like everything I did was wrong and I was a target of their anger, fear, and hostility. As a result, my personal progress became *frozen*—if anything I did seemed wrong, the only right thing to do was nothing. This caucus was the first opportunity I have had to explore how I really feel about diversity and other groups in the company of others like myself. As a result, I believe I am beginning to get it. What women, people of color, and homo/bisexuals need for me to do is to create the space for them to be themselves, with their unique and collective strengths to make life better for all of us.

—Al

For twenty years I have read white men's personal reflections. I am always struck by their sincerity and depth of learning. I consider myself lucky to get to facilitate this work. It's work Bill and I both love and feel called to do in the world.

One of my mentors is Mark Chesler. For my dissertation, I'd interviewed eight white men on their life journeys of learning about diversity. Mark inspired me when he ended his interview by saying, "The only way to touch other white men is through love." His words have always stayed with me. However, the overall pattern observed in my dissertation was that white male diversity advocates disconnected from other white men and drew most of their support from white women and people of color. They were frustrated and angry toward other white men. Mark's words reinforced the journey Bill and I have gone on—to love the white male part of ourselves and to love the white male part of the men we work with.

I later learned Mark's definition of love stemmed from his Jewish background, which meant love included not simply acceptance but also challenge. He differentiated that from a Christian version of love, which to him was simply unconditional love. That was one of the notions that inspired our paradox of support accompanied by challenge. As I looked around the room in our final hours, I was aware of how much support and challenge had driven the deep and profound learning the men were now reflecting. The sense of love among the men in the room was also palpable.

Recently I was listening to a talk by John Powell, an expert on race. I was struck by his perspective that people have more confidence in expressing fear and anger than they do in expressing love:

> We don't have confidence in love. . . . We have much more confidence in anger and hate. We believe anger is powerful. We believe hate is powerful. And we believe love is wimpy. And so if we're engaged in the world, we believe it's much better to sort of organize around anger and hate.

John goes on to speak about Nelson Mandela as someone who had confidence in love. I realize now I don't just carry Nelson Mandela's love toward engaging white men—I also carry his confidence in love. It's not enough to operate from a place of love; we must also believe in the power of love.

Recently my older daughter spent a high school semester in Southwest Africa as part of a study abroad program with The Traveling School. Her group consisted of fifteen girls and four women faculty. One day they visited with anti-apartheid activist Denis Goldberg at his house in Cape Town. He cooked them a meal and talked with them about his life. The only white man to be convicted of treason alongside his close colleague Nelson Mandela in the Rivonia Trial, Denis spent twenty-two years in prison. His new biography is appropriately titled *A Life for Freedom*.

Connected through my daughter, Denis and I have corresponded by email. He told me that he came out of prison saying, "When apartheid is defeated, whites will be free to be human in their interactions with everyone else, including among whites themselves." According to Denis, Nelson Mandela also spoke about how whites would be "free to be free." I resonate deeply with this concept of becoming free. Over and over in the last twenty years I have seen white men look in the mirror at their own biases, privileges, and cultural constraints. Ultimately, through that journey, we discover new layers of our own freedom. It is ironic that when white men look at the parts of themselves that they may least want to explore, they are unexpectedly deeply moved and gain a newfound sense of freedom. Two of the reasons the White Men's Caucus is so often described as life changing for white men is due to our trust in love as the way to engage, and the powerful impact of becoming *free to be free*.

It was time to support the men in transferring their learning back to work and home. Bill and I both stood and walked over to different flipcharts.

"What are some of the tools and skills you have learned

this week that you can take back with you?" I asked while posed to capture some notes.

Frank jumped in first. "I learned what it truly means to listen. It's not about listening to *fix* or listening to *debate*. It's about truly trying to understand another person's world. For me it's also about suspending the need to be right. I can shift my focus from telling to listening, from advocacy to inquiry."

"That's a huge shift for you, Frank," said Al. "Your co-workers are still used to you being General Frankie."

Giggles filled the room.

"All it took was us all holding you down to the floor for you to shift," said Joe smiling. "That's all. And by the way, you're welcome."

"Thanks," said Frank with a grin.

I was happy to hear Frank own several of the radical habits and leadership skills.

"For me the paradoxes are a huge tool to take back," said Lee. "I can help other white guys see the complexities of diversity. Seeing the world from an either/or lens is limiting. I like the statement that my view of the world isn't *wrong*; more likely it is *incomplete*. Treating everyone the same and being color blind may seem like a simple solution, but it forces everyone to fit into our white male version of sameness."

"I agree with that," said Joe. "One of the tools for me is suspending the problem-solving mode to let things *sit and sink in*. I can actively explore my discomfort rather than trying to avoid discomfort and ambiguity."

"What about allowing silence in the group, Joe?" I asked.

"I hated that for a long time, but I have come to appreciate our times of silence," said Joe. "I also see value in lots of the self-reflection modes we have used, whether it's journaling, talking one on one, even talking to my wife at night about all this."

"What other tools do you want to take with you?" asked Bill.

"I feel like I have more permission to use my heart," said Al. "I can step out of the white male culture of *rationality over emotion* and share my heart. It doesn't mean I'm weak. Rather, it gives others permission to be human and connect at that level too."

I felt joy in hearing about Al's sense of freedom.

I moved on. "Now I have another question. This is one you couldn't have answered the first day. What's in it for white men to be on this journey of exploring and advocating for diversity? What's our self-interest?"

"You mean: why is it good for the business?" asked Joe.

"Let's make it more personal than that," I said. "Remember some of the assumptions about white men and diversity that surfaced at the beginning of the week? Such as the assumption that diversity is a zero sum game and if others gain, we lose? Now that you have journeyed through the week, maybe you can see how others can gain through diversity *and* we can too."

"That's another shift to *both/and*, rather than an *either/ or*," stated Lee.

I wrote WIIFWM at the top of flipchart page, which stood for *What's in It for White Men*. In a few minutes we had brainstormed a list.

WHAT'S IN IT FOR WHITE MEN?

- ► I gain better self-awareness. (I understand the water I swim in.)

- ► I can have more honest and authentic conversations and relationships.

- ► I can have more support from other white men and less isolation. It's okay to ask for help.

- ► This work helps me have better communication at home as I listen differently and focus on understanding and connecting.

- ► This has reduced my feelings of guilt or shame.

- ► I have more permission to be human and an enhanced willingness to show and work with emotion.

- ► This work helps me be more comfortable with being a white male, since it's now something that has been examined.

- ► It makes it fun to go to work, more harmonious.

- ► I can actually make a difference to move us forward as an organization by using my new self-awareness.

- ► I gain greater curiosity and willingness to learn and ask questions.

- ► People will see that I have an open mind and want to join my team.

- ► I can understand others better, and others can understand me better.

- ► We will foster better idea sharing at work and thus better decision making for the organization.

- ► I have more willingness to show vulnerability and make mistakes in service to my learning.

- ► I've expanded my leadership style.

- ► I will waste less time walking on eggshells around these topics.

- ► I am more open to change now and can see messiness and turbulence as an opportunity to grow critical leadership skills.

"This list really does blow up the myth that white men lose with diversity," said Joe.

"The truth is it's more about everybody winning," said Lee.

"Sometimes we say that white men actually have as much or more to gain from diversity than any other group," said Bill, "because we typically have the least awareness of the water we swim in. We have the most room to learn and grow."

"Sometimes we apply an assumption of zero sum or finiteness to something that is actually infinite," I said. "If I have a lit candle and I light your candle, that doesn't mean mine goes out. Yet we often assume that by being more inclusive of others, we are giving up something. Which brings us to another radical habit shift in our thinking."

MINDSET #11

Notice abundance rather than assume scarcity. When our worldview is one of scarcity, we succumb to fear and struggle. Yes, some resources are finite, but others are infinite. Share the wealth.

It is possible to create space for inclusion of everyone. Resources such as love, creativity, connection, and learning are infinite. Whenever I take the time to remember this truth, I find my body relax and I feel excitement for the future.

Bill shifted the group's gears forward. "I want each of you to spend twenty minutes alone to start creating an action plan—one or two next steps as you leave here to apply or continue your learning. There is a template to use in your workbook. After twenty minutes spend another thirty minutes over lunch with a colleague sharing your action plans and coaching each other. You will be following up with each other once you're back home, so make a plan to touch base in a few weeks."

The men identified their new action-planning partner while I started taking pictures of all the flipcharts on the wall so that our office could transcribe the lab notes to email back to the guys in about a week.

TWENTY-ONE

Closing and Looking Forward

WE RECONVENED BY TAKING A GROUP PHOTO OUT ON the deck. The guys prodded us to take a few pictures of them peering over the deck at Snappy, who looked unenthused. No one volunteered to go down to the water for a close-up next to the 300-pound snapping turtle.

We took some time for some of the guys to report out their action plans. Then we shifted to a caucus activity that is a favorite of Bill's and mine. Bill placed two chairs facing each other in the middle of the circle.

"One of the best ways to be ready to have conversations about what this week was about is to actually practice," said Bill. "Who would like to go out and practice talking about this session with someone back at work? Perhaps it's another white guy who is skeptical about what this experience is all about."

Frank stood up and moved to one of the chairs in the circle. He appeared to be in deep thought. He let out a sigh as he spoke up. "Actually, I want to practice having a conversation with my son."

The room was quiet. No one, even Bill and I, had expected this.

"Do you want to play yourself, Frank?" asked Bill. "Or do you want to play your son and see how other guys might approach this?"

"I want to play myself," said Frank.

"Who is willing to help Frank by playing his son in this role play?" asked Bill.

Al and Lee both stood up at the same time. I was struck by how powerful it would be for either of them. Lee could have an opportunity to have a father who was present rather than the absent dad he experienced. Al could have an opportunity to have a gentler father than the one he had, which he had seen Frank model the day before in the role play. I realized I wanted both of them in that other chair. Al and Lee regarded each other for a moment.

Al sat back down in his chair and motioned for Lee to continue.

"I want to see you have a father, Lee," said Al. "Even if it's just a role play."

Lee and Frank sat in chairs facing each other, a few feet apart. Frank's face was softer than usual.

"Okay, so try a few minutes, Frank," said Bill.

"Hi, son," said Frank. "I've been reflecting on the last week. You came home last week and you told me you were being bullied at school. I know I got upset because you were crying. I told you to suck it up and stop crying."

Lee was motionless as he took in what it was like to have the attention of a dad who wanted to talk to his son. I think it was a new experience for him.

"Yeah, Dad," said Lee. "I remember quite well."

"Well, I was wrong to say that," said Frank. "You don't need to suck it up. In fact, whenever you are feeling anything like that, I want you to come to me, and I will listen and be there for you."

Frank looked relieved. I saw Lee's eyes water.

"Thanks, Dad," said Lee as he hung his head for a second and scratched his neck. "Sometimes I just don't know what to do when the other guys pick on me. I feel like a loser and I also get so mad inside."

Frank said nothing for a bit. I sat there hoping he didn't jump into trying-to-fix-the-problem mode at the expense of simply being present.

To his credit, Frank chose the latter. "I'm sorry, son," he said. "You shouldn't be treated like that. What can I do to help?"

Lee let out a big sigh, like he had never been asked that before, and a few years of stress disappeared from his face.

"How about just us hanging out together," said Lee with a hopeful expression.

"You got it. You shouldn't have to ask me to spend time with you, son," said Frank. "I ought to already be doing that. And I'm sorry that I haven't."

I felt a tear in my eye, and I noticed a few other tears around the room.

"Let's pause it there," said Bill.

Frank and Lee stood up and embraced briefly.

"Nice work, Frank," said Lee.

"Let's take a few minutes to share what you noticed about that role play," said Bill.

"I wish my dad could have made the shift that I just saw you make," said Al as he wiped a tear from his eye. "You're a different man than yesterday's role play, Frank."

"Frank," said Joe. "You showed up ready to be present and connect with your son. He opened up to you. I think you'll do great when you go home. Even if you waver occasionally, like anything you set your mind to, you will succeed in the long term. I want to know how it goes. "

"Thanks, guys," said Frank.

"How about another role play?" asked Bill. "Any of you guys need to talk to a skeptical white guy when you go back?"

All of the men were nodding.

Joe jumped out of his rocking chair and sat in one of the middle chairs. The men cheered him on for volunteering.

"What is the situation, Joe?" I asked.

"It's just as you said," answered Joe. "A white male colleague who is very skeptical of this diversity stuff."

"Do you want to play him?" I said.

"Sure," said Joe. A grin came across his face, and he rubbed his hands together.

Al went out to the other chair. "Okay, I'll give it a try," he said.

Joe and Al stared at each other, waiting for the other to start.

"So, how was white men's camp?" said Joe, as he stared hard at Al.

The guys roared. They were on the edge of their seats. Perhaps they all knew that question was waiting for them back at home.

"Aah," started Al, perhaps caught a little off guard. "It was a lot different from what I thought. I wondered if I had done something wrong to get sent there. And I also thought to myself: what could I possibly learn about diversity from a bunch of white guys? But I did learn much more than I expected. As white guys, we do have a different experience in the world than women or people of color. For example, do you know how often women wonder about their personal safety, Joe?"

Al was off to a good start here, speaking personally from the heart. Many white guys return and try to preach everything they learned at once.

"I think you drank the Kool-Aid, Al," said Joe. "I mean, don't you think we have taken this diversity thing too far, with all these employee resource groups? Those seem divisive to me. Where is the white male employee group? How come we don't have a month focused on us?"

"You didn't answer my question, Joe," said Al. "How often do you think about your own safety compared to most women?"

"I think about my safety all the time as a cop," said Joe. "But I know my wife thinks about it in many ways that I don't."

"Does anyone look at you and think or say you got your job because you're a white guy?" said Al. "No one does that about me. Yet people of color are accused of getting their job because of their color and feel like they have to work twice as hard to prove they're qualified."

Joe gazed at Al with reflection.

The most difficult conversation for most white guys who have been through the White Men's Caucus is to engage other white men. The conversations with white women and people of color can be challenging but are often rewarding. It is another aspect of our privilege, to choose whether and how to engage other white guys around diversity. Most often the burden to educate other white men is left to people of color, white women, and other groups. Organizational cultures will truly shift their inclusion when white guys begin to engage other white guys on this topic. Especially with those who are harder to sell. Many men go back to work to find the very same skepticism they'd brought to the caucus themselves. While they've had four days to reflect and develop their thinking, it can be overwhelming to try to convey their shift in mindsets to other guys.

Joe leaned toward Al. "Some of the people of color you are defending are just playing the race card, Al. Don't you see that? They actually have it easier. My neighbor's son got higher scores on the SAT than kids of color down the block. But it was the kids of color who got accepted, even though the white kid had higher scores. That just isn't fair."

Al wiped a bead of sweat off his brow. Clearly Joe was doing a good job playing the cynical white guy back at work.

I saw Bill glance at the clock and nod to me. I wrapped up the second role play, and we spent a few minutes debriefing it. Then it was time for our last activity.

"We are going to take some time to do something we don't often get a chance to do," I said.

"Not again," said Frank, perhaps referring to the nonverbal nurturing exercise.

"Often in our white male culture we are focused on problem solving and have a critical lens, focusing on what's wrong. We are going to shift to examining what we appreciate. We are going to practice another radical thought habit shift."

MINDSET #12

Notice, appreciate, and acknowledge what is working well. Our strong problem-solving muscle has us often looking to address what's wrong in order to solve it. Put your attention on what you want to grow.

"As we wind down, let's take some time to express any appreciations and acknowledgments you may have for each other," I said. "Look around the room and notice who has impacted you in some significant way. Let them know that."

The group got quiet for a moment.

Frank leaned over toward Al. "I'm so glad we did this caucus together, Al," said Frank. "We've worked together for twenty years, and I've gotten to know you more in these four days than all the rest of our years combined. I'm really proud of the courage I see growing in you. Hell, you've always had courage, I just think back to you provoking your dad so he wouldn't abuse your brothers."

Frank paused, slightly choked up.

"I've witnessed you here free of the need for others to like you," Frank continued. "I'm excited about that. Our company needs your skills, including your heart that you are now giving yourself more permission to use. And I want to be whatever support I can in your struggle with the depression you spoke of yesterday."

Al nodded and let out a sigh. "Thank you, Frank," he said.

"I said the first day that sometimes I just want to stay to my introverted self," said Lee. "But here I have relearned that my voice really counts. Thank you to you strong extroverts, Joe and Frank, for listening. It felt good to hear your positive reflections on the uncle and father I am being." Lee paused. "I also appreciate our silence."

The men sat without speaking for a minute.

"And, Joe," started Lee, "thank you for apologizing for what was done to me by that group of boys when I was younger. It helps me deal with the isolation I felt in high school from being teased and ostracized when I spoke out against the homophobic bullying."

Joe nodded.

"You have done a good job, Joe, of leaving behind your either/or thinking and wading into the ambiguity here," said Lee. "I think that will serve you well."

"Lee," said Joe. "I really appreciate your having my back and helping me with the TV reporter."

"You bet," said Lee. "Let's go back home and see what they are saying about us now. If they only knew how worthwhile our time has been."

"Any other appreciations?" I asked.

Bill spoke, "Thanks, Frank, for bringing your skepticism, which, in my opinion, added to our conversation."

Al leaned back over to Frank. "You have changed so much this week. I feel like I have a new colleague. That role play with your son said it all. I think you are going to have a whole different kind of partnering with your folks at work. I actually can't wait to go to work with you. I didn't honestly feel that way before."

Frank smiled, content.

"Bill," I said, "I want to acknowledge you for dreaming up and then courageously piloting the first White Men's Caucus back in 1997. It was a bold thing to try. It is a privilege, and a good one at that, to be able to partner with you for more than twenty years. I feel in many ways like you are the brother that I never had, having grown up with five sisters."

Bill's face flushed. "Michael, I want to publically acknowledge how much it means to me that you always have my back," said Bill. "This whole journey continues to be truly a grand adventure, and partnering with you has always been natural and easy."

As I rocked in the chair I savored the moment. The journey that all of us in the room had just traveled was significant, as were the gifts that each of us would take away to improve our relationships at work, as well as at home and with families.

"Good work, guys. We are complete," I said. "Safe travels, everyone." The men slowly rose to shake hands and hug each other before departing. I was glad they had all had taken us up on our offer for a follow-up group coaching call one month out.

TWENTY-TWO

Four Weeks Later

IN THE FOUR WEEKS SINCE THE CAUCUS ENDED, THE memories of Snappy and our group together have started to fade. The month of May has arrived, and with it, full-on springtime. It was the day for our follow-up call with the men from last month's caucus. We have recently been offering follow-up group coaching to support guys in further integration and application of their learning.

To get reoriented, I sat at my computer and pulled up the one email I had received after the caucus. It was from Frank, and he sent it the night the caucus ended.

Guys,

I want to thank you again for this week. As I fly home I've been reflecting on what I am going to do. I'm up to four pages of notes to start implementing next week. Quite frankly, this was the best training I have ever been to. You guys will always be in my heart and my mind. I haven't felt this energized in ten years. I didn't know the openness and sharing of insights we had was even possible at a work event. Thank you for enabling me to be not only a better leader but a better human being.

Sincerely, Frank

I felt excitement as I dialed into the conference number.

"Hello, this is Snappy," I said with an odd accent.

I heard a roar from the guys on the phone.

"Actually this is Michael," I explained. "Who's on the call?"

"This is Frank and Al," reported Frank. "We are sitting in my office together."

Lee, Joe, and Bill also reported being on the call.

"Great to hear your voices," I said. "Who wants to check in first on how it's been going?"

"I'll share," said Joe. "I was only home thirty seconds before my wife said, 'You've changed.'"

"Wow," said Lee. "That didn't take her long to notice."

"Well, you guys know I do like to dish out the banter with the guys," continued Joe. "I realized I also do that to my wife, and she doesn't like that. So I stopped. Now she literally wants to know who to send the thank-you card to."

I smiled, knowing that companies have actually gotten thank-you cards from spouses of white male executives. One wife wrote: "I don't know what you did to my husband, but frankly I don't want the old husband back." Another called her company to ask a question about benefits and mentioned that her husband was much more patient with her children since returning from the White Men's Caucus.

"My wife likes that I am more comfortable with silence," said Joe. "I also receive her occasional crying and don't assume she's weak or needs my problem solving. It's just her way of processing. We had a very heartfelt conversation one evening about why she sought out jaw surgery. I talked about beginning to understand the world of sexual objectification and the narrow beauty standards women live in. She appreciated that I now know more about that societal pressure on her. It's a complicated world, and I am actually more okay being confused about it all."

"How's your son?" asked Lee.

"He's doing okay," said Joe. "Well, he hasn't gotten worse. I'm embracing the mystery of his disease, and I am more okay not knowing the future. What's different is that I am more at ease enjoying every moment with him. I feel more connected to him. I actually asked him 'What's it like to be you?' I don't know why I never thought of asking anyone that question before. What he shared was amazing to hear."

"That's more of a *being* question than a *doing* question, Joe," I said. "It's not a question that our action-oriented, critical-analysis, future-focused, or bantering white male–culture style of communicating would lead us to ask."

I flashed back to the many weekends I've spent over the past three years learning a process called Circling at the Integral Center in Boulder, Colorado. That is where I learned to ask questions like Joe's. Circling is a process of exploring and getting a person's world. The intent is to celebrate and appreciate who they are at that point, rather than trying to fix or change them. It's my favorite way to get out of the *doing* mode and shift into *being* with others. Getting certified in Circling enhanced my ability to slow down, be curious, and notice what it's like to be with someone. I find I am much more likely to create shared understanding. An edge for me was learning that a strong sense of connection does not just come from listening, rather more from sharing the impact of what it's like for me to be with that person. I can simply own my experience of how I am impacted in that instant and share it. One way to know if you are owning your experience is if it can't be argued. This type of authentic relating has opened my world, and I have enjoyed bringing these practices into my caucuses and Allies Labs, my community, my men's group, my daughter's high school, my family, and even my dad's family reunion. Circling incorporates many of the twelve radical thought habits. I imagined myself sitting in front of Joe.

"When I hear your story I feel lucky to know you and inspired to connect even more with my own family," I said to Joe, speaking in a way that I'd learned was owning my experience. "What else, Joe?" I added.

"I apologized to my older brother for trying to toughen him up and making it harder for him to come out to me," said Joe. "I think we may end up closer than we have ever been before. So, in terms of work, I've had some great breakthroughs. I definitely do more listening to employees and let them identify solutions rather than imposing my own. Remember my African American colleague who I said often seemed angry? My first conversation with him didn't change things much. I think it was after he saw me publicly discussing with other white cops what I'd learned about white privilege that he started opening up to me. I knew he was isolated, but I had no idea how hard it really was for him. I've been making sure his voice is heard in our shift meetings. We have also attended each other's churches, and we watched the movie *42*, the film about Jackie Robinson becoming the first black major league baseball player. But the hardest thing is still to talk with other skeptical white guys. I still am on a learning curve there."

"You're not alone, Joe," said Bill. "That is often the hardest part of this work. We are the ones who should be stepping up to educate our white male colleagues. So keep leaning into that. Just be yourself and share your learning journey."

"Any more TV reporters crashing in on your meetings?" I asked.

"Nope," said Joe. "That quickly faded away after the caucus. But I did present on a panel at a Racial Equity in Government Conference. Someone asked me whether I understand white privilege. I think they were skeptical. I told them that my son had recently asked me why there were riots against the police on TV. Then I told the 800 people at the conference what I told my son and how I had learned that at the White Men's Caucus. I also told them what I would have told my son before I had gone to the caucus. People seemed shocked. They didn't expect that from me. It really does inspire hope from others when we share from the heart about our caucus learning. We all have to keep talking about this."

"I actually heard from another client of ours who was at that conference," I added. "You really did impact them. My client said you could have heard a pin drop. I feel grateful that you were willing to be so personal in what you shared." Everyone paused on the phone, perhaps also impacted by Joe's story.

"How about you, Lee?" I asked, wanting to hear from our introvert sooner rather than later.

"I've gotten active in our women's network," said Lee. "Actually, here is another story. I was at a performance-rating and succession-planning meeting recently. We were discussing four guys and one woman. I couldn't believe no one was advocating for the woman. I knew she was the most qualified. Yet none of my male colleagues were speaking up for her. It was just like some of the dynamics we talked about at the caucus."

"So what did you do?" Bill asked.

"I finally spoke up and said I think she is the most qualified," said Lee. "I also said it's interesting that she is the only woman and no one is speaking up for her."

"How did that go over?" said Bill.

"Initially they denied that, but eventually one of the guys said maybe there was something to that," said Lee. "I think they will all be more conscious now.

"I also led a lunch discussion on introverts in the workplace, after showing Susan Cain's TED Talk called 'The Power of Introverts,'" said Lee. "It was extremely popular, and I have been asked to do more of those sessions."

"That's great, Lee," said Frank. "I wish you could do that in my organization."

"I'm sure you can find a few introverts who can do that, Frank," said Lee. "Oh, and I did have a great conversation with my niece about my caucus learning. She ended the conversation by thanking me for being there as her uncle." He paused. "I thought about reaching out to my father," said

Lee. "But I haven't." His voice trailed off, and another pause followed.

"Lee, call me if you want to talk through that some more," said Frank.

"Okay," said Lee. "I will call you. Thanks."

"I have no interest in reaching out to my dad," blurted out Al. "But I did call my daughter, whom I haven't spoken to in two years."

"What happened?" asked Lee.

"She still wouldn't talk to me," said Al. "So I wrote her a letter owning how I distanced myself from her when she reached puberty."

Everyone kept listening as we waited for Al to continue.

"I've stopped the objectification of women that I spoke about during the caucus," said Al. "I actually have called out other men when I've seen them eyeballing women."

"I can vouch for that," said Frank. "Al's more of an alpha male with the guys around here. He isn't out looking for approval—including my approval."

Frank's last words had both a playful and annoyed tone. Perhaps he still had mixed feelings about regularly being challenged by Al.

"You have met your match, Frank," said Joe. "So what about you, Frank?"

"Well," said Frank. "Where do I begin? I listen much more to my colleagues at work."

My mind flashed to the two recent Catalyst studies (referred to in the introduction) that researched the impact of our White Men's Caucuses and White Men & Allies

Learning Labs on leaders at Rockwell Automation. The first report, *Calling All White Men: Can Training Help Create Inclusive Workplaces?*, found that co-workers rated white men 31 percent higher on inquiring across difference after the lab. Men noticeably improved at asking questions of people different from themselves. That is a remarkable change after just four days. There was also a significant drop in workplace gossip and a significant increase in four other inclusive behaviors. The second study, *Anatomy of Change: How Inclusive Cultures Evolve*, confirmed the organizational culture itself was impacted. So I knew what Frank was saying was true.

"Tell them about your conversation with Joan," said Al.

"Turns out she was pretty irritated with me," said Frank.

"No surprise," said Lee.

"In our second conversation, after I shared some of my ahas from the caucus, she confirmed that she felt like I didn't take her seriously," continued Frank. "I've committed to building a real partnership with her. Al is also coaching me on this."

"That sounds like a good start, Frank," said Bill.

"Oh, and I've stopped answering email on weekends, and I also hired a female admin," said Frank.

"Tell them where you went last night," said Al.

"I want to the LGBT resource group meeting," said Frank.

"Wow," said Lee.

"What about connecting with your spouses, Frank and Al?" I asked. "How has that gone?"

I was curious because I've heard plenty of anecdotes

that the 31-percent increase in listening happens for guys at home too. It reminds me of how basic shifts in behaviors can make profound differences in marriages and partnerships that can be quite observable. For instance, researcher John Gottman found that he can, after listening to a couple for five minutes, predict with 91 percent accuracy whether they will remain married six years later. His research applies to partners regardless of sexual orientation. He found that partners make requests for connections, which he calls *bids*. The other partner can either turn toward, ignore, or turn away from the bid. Couples who divorced within six years had turn-toward bids 33 percent of the time, which means that only three in ten bids for emotional connection were met with intimacy. The couples still together after six years had turn-toward bids 87 percent of the time. This translates to partners meeting those emotional needs nine times out of ten.

Ironically, years earlier, when I studied Keith Johnstone's book *Impro: Improvisation and the Theatre*, I found a similar pattern. Rather than calling them *bids* he calls them *offers*. An improvisational actor constantly puts out offers, and other actors are trained to accept each other's offers and build on them. One actor may point to the sky and gasp. If the second actor looks up at the sky and reacts, she has accepted the first actor's offer. The people watching are not used to so much offer acceptance, and that's what makes the audience excited and amused. Couples build on the same energy by accepting each other's bids. I wondered if there was a shift in Frank's and Al's connections with their spouses, similar to what Joe described. I know that when guys apply their caucus learning to their home life, they automatically apply it to their work life.

"I am determined not to let my second marriage end in divorce," said Frank. "I think the radical habits and leadership skills are going to be great tools to make my marriage work. I do listen much more. She has really noticed I am willing to be in my heart and share what's real to me. Once in a while I digress into problem solving or not listening, but the bar is set higher and she holds me accountable. What's nice is that I now talk to my office neighbor Al about all this stuff, and he challenges me to stay on track."

"I'm glad you have that support," said Bill. "What about you, Al?"

"Honestly, I think I came close to a divorce a few weeks ago," said Al.

The men were quiet on the phone as they waited for more details.

"I talked to my wife about my objectification of women at work," said Al. "She didn't realize the extent of it and was not happy. I asked about and apologized for how that impacted our relationship. I also apologized for how I just wasn't present for the kids when I worked so much in the past."

"Did things get more stable?" I asked.

"She seemed to sense I have a new confidence, that I don't need her approval. She likes that. So, yeah, things are on the way up again."

"Frank, what about your son?" asked Lee. "The one you practiced your role play about?"

"That went great," said Frank. "Actually I was nervous, but I said essentially the same things I did in our role play, which really helped, by the way. He seems to want to spend more time with me. I'm going to reach out to my older son, too, this month."

"I feel inspired hearing all of you courageously apply your learning from the White Men's Caucus," I said.

The white men from this caucus dove fully into examining what it means to be white, male, and heterosexual. Through those insights they found a deeper way to relate to each other. They also discovered a new freedom to own parts of themselves that the white male culture discourages. They became more whole, while still connecting to and loving the white male part of themselves. They grew more open to see the world in new ways. They grew the courage to be vulnerable, more authentic, and more human. They found new ways to connect more with each other and others in the world. As I pondered this I felt a strong sense of hope that the future for white men and everyone in this world is bright.

The 12 Radical Habits
(New Mindsets)

MINDSET #1: It no longer works to see everything in life as a problem to solve. Life is a journey in which new questions and perspectives arise. The journey itself will lead to more profound learning.

MINDSET #2: Incorporate multiple perspectives, even if they are contradictory. They give you a more intricate view of the world. Seeing the world from only one perspective gives an incomplete view.

MINDSET #3: Your strengths overused become weaknesses. Notice when your strengths don't serve you. Create the space to grow underutilized skills and attributes even if you feel tentative at first.

MINDSET #4: Learn to accept ambiguity, emotion, and discomfort.

MINDSET #5: Inquire and seek the insights of others. Maximizing inquiry will expand learning and create new partnerships. Most of us spend an overwhelming majority of our time in advocacy, arguing our positions and proving that our views are right. There is another way.

MINDSET #6: Focus on the present to create immediate and deeper connection—with yourself and others. Our focus is often on creating the future or examining the past while neglecting the present.

MINDSET #7: Recognize we are all in this together. Discover our interdependence. Our interconnectedness is more critical to our ultimate survival as a species than any sense of independence that may resonate with you now.

MINDSET #8: Explore just *being*, and step out of *doing*. We often assume our essential value comes from focusing on action and getting things done. But acting without reflection can derail success. New paths open when we take the time to just *be*.

MINDSET #9: Show up with vulnerability—it's a form of courage. You'll create more openness and deeper connections than ever before.

MINDSET #10: Be conscious of intent and impact. By tuning into both the intent and impact we have on each other, we build a foundation for full partnership.

MINDSET #11: Notice abundance rather than assume scarcity. When our worldview is one of scarcity, we succumb to fear and tend to struggle. Yes, some resources are finite, but others are infinite. Share the wealth.

MINDSET #12: Notice, appreciate, and acknowledge what is working well. Our strong problem-solving muscle has us often looking to address what's wrong in order to solve it. Put your attention on what you want to grow.

Eight Critical Leadership Skills: A Self-Rating

Below are six behaviors for each of the Eight Critical Leadership Skills. For each behavior, rate yourself on a 1–5 scale (1 = low, 5 = high). Assess yourself realistically, based on how you would demonstrate the behaviors. Then look back and select three behaviors you want to focus on strengthening.

COURAGE

— I visibly demonstrate the principles that are most important to me.

— I choose to act on my beliefs and fears, aware of the risks involved.

— I own my discomfort and acknowledge what I am feeling.

— I enlist others in answering difficult questions and say I don't know when necessary.

— I act to create change by speaking my truth, even when doing so may cause discomfort or conflict.

— I consistently speak my truth in a way that acknowledges it as *my* perspective, not the *only* perspective.

INTEGRATING HEAD AND HEART

— I value and demonstrate feelings (from the heart) as well as knowledge, thoughts, and concepts (from the head).

— I show vulnerability that allows openness and authentic connections with others.

— I am able to talk about diversity and inclusion from my personal perspective.

— I respond using both my head and heart as the situation requires.

— I acknowledge my blind spots when I become aware of them.

— I validate others' viewpoints whether I agree with them or not.

LISTENING

— I repeat back the essence of others' perspectives, so they know I hear them.

— I listen to others' perspectives without interrupting to defend or clarify my own position.

— I actively learn about my colleagues—who they really are.

— I notice and successfully control my reflex to debate instead of listening.

— I recognize the difference between listening to solve a problem and listening to understand, and I am willing to ask which one is needed.

BALANCING KEY PARADOXES

— I use a "both/and" mindset that allows for multiple viewpoints or options.

— I am able to see contradictory goals and needs as equally valid.

— I ask open-ended questions that help me learn new perspectives and think more broadly.

— I recognize when a situation is less a problem to be solved and more a paradox to be managed.

— I validate the perspectives of others even when perspectives are contradictory to my own.

— I realize that my ability to see and apply both sides of a paradox is important to my success as a leader.

LEVERAGING AMBIGUITY AND TURBULENCE

— I acknowledge when I'm confused, rather than try to change what is confusing.

— I manage my own and others' discomfort with uncertainty and change.

— I don't wait to get everything right before taking action. I can take action before I feel fully prepared.

— I am able to resist the urge to oversimplify situations, and I work through complex issues with an open mind.

— I lean into discomfort as a way to deepen my learning and understanding.

— I display patience with conflict and recognize its potential to bring about productive change.

MANAGING DIFFICULT CONVERSATIONS

— I initiate direct, honest, and timely conversations.

— I acknowledge when something is not working and search for a better approach/outcome.

— I stay aware of my assumptions and stereotypes to avoid dismissing and invalidating others' perspectives.

— When listening, I recognize when I am just observing behavior and when I am attributing to another my own interpretation of their behavior.

— I recognize the difference between my intentions when interacting with others and how I may have a different impact than intended.

— I do not use lack of time as an excuse to avoid difficult conversations.

SEEING AND THINKING SYSTEMICALLY

— I understand I am part of many different diversity groups and that this affects both my experience of the world and how others see me.

— I understand unconscious bias and systemic privilege and the way it affects how I hear others and how they hear me.

— I understand that my view of a situation is incomplete until I understand the perspectives of the other people involved.

— I notice and understand how inequities of systemic privilege—from race, class, gender, or other factors— impact how I assess and interact with others.

— I recognize when someone is talking to me as an individual or as a member of a diversity group.

— I encourage people throughout the organization to pay attention to issues of privilege, bias, and inclusion at work.

BEING AN AGENT OF CHANGE

— I encourage others to see new possibilities and take action.

— I accept change as a never-ending process in all parts of my life.

— I model creating inclusion, ownership, and commitment while implementing change.

— I build commitment to new approaches rather than imposing compliance.

— I recognize that when I commit to being a change agent, I am going to change too.

For more, see Michael Welp, Jo Ann Morris, and Bill Proudman, *Eight Critical Leadership Skills Created Through Effective Diversity Partnerships* (3rd ed.). Portland, OR: White Men as Full Diversity Partners, 2015.

Note: An online leadership skills 360-assessment process is available through WMFDP.

Catalyst Press Release

Research on the impact of the White Men's Caucus and the Allies Learning Lab is documented in this press release from Catalyst:

CATALYST STUDY SHOWS TRAINING FOR WHITE MEN KEY TO IMPROVING WORKPLACE CULTURE

NEW YORK—Can training really make corporate cultures dominated by white men more inclusive? For years, critics have debated its impact, but a new Catalyst study with employees of the global engineering company Rockwell Automation, *Calling All White Men: Can Training Help Create Inclusive Workplaces?* shows training can produce a measurable shift in workplace attitudes and behavior—and begin to create an environment where women and minorities can advance.

Catalyst surveyed Rockwell employees—mostly white male managers—who participated in leadership development programs run by the organization White Men as Full Diversity Partners. In an industry dominated by white men, Rockwell hoped the programs would equip and inspire its white male employees to play a more central leadership role in creating an inclusive work environment.

The study supports Catalyst's belief in the importance of engaging men as champions of gender diversity. Catalyst recently launched MARC—Men Advocating Real Change—an online learning community for professionals committed to achieving gender equality in the workplace.

Key findings of the Catalyst study include:

An increase in workplace civility and decline in gossip (e.g., snide remarks and behind-the-back comments). In some workgroups, participants' colleagues rated the incidence of workplace gossip as much as 39 percent lower after the labs, signaling improved communication and respect.

Managers were more likely to acknowledge that inequities exist. After the labs, there was a 17 percent increase in how much managers agreed that white men have greater advantages than women and racial/ethnic minorities.

Managers improved on five key behaviors for inclusion. From seeking out varied perspectives to becoming more direct in addressing emotionally charged matters, managers improved on critical skills for leading in today's diverse marketplace.

Having cross-racial friendships mattered. Managers without many prior cross-racial relationships changed the most after the labs when it came to thinking critically about different social groups—a 40 percent increase in ratings vs. a 9 percent increase for those with more of these relationships.

Those who cared the least about exhibiting prejudice changed the most. After the labs, managers who initially were the least concerned about appearing prejudiced were the ones who registered the most significant change in taking personal responsibility for being inclusive, as evidenced by a 15 percent increase in ratings.

"Companies can see a major shift in inclusive behavior when white men acknowledge inequalities and accept that while they didn't cause the problem, it's their responsibility as leaders to be part of the solution," said Ilene H. Lang, President and former CEO of Catalyst. "We can't rely only on women and minorities to advocate for culture change. The results are much more powerful when white men, who are most often in leadership positions, are also role models."

From http://www.catalyst.org/media/calling-all-white-men, July 2012.

Other links about this Catalyst research report:

http://blogs.wsj.com/atwork/2012/07/18/a-little-diversity-training -goes-a-long-way/

http://www.hreonline.com/HRE/view/story.jhtml?id=533350089

Catalyst is a global nonprofit research organization headquartered in New York that has been researching gender in corporations for more than fifty years. Many other resources are available on Catalyst's website (www.catalyst.org) and on its dedicated website for MARC: Men Advocating for Real Change (http://onthemarc .org).

Letter to Nelson Mandela

September 6, 2010

Dear Nelson Mandela,

This is a letter of thank you for who you are and what you stand for, and to let you know the impact you have had on my life, and the resulting impact I am now having on many others' lives.

In September 1990 I came to live and work in South Africa and Lesotho for almost a year, drawn by your freedom in February 1990. At that time you had been in prison essentially my whole life, beginning within a year of my birth in 1962.

Only in my two years prior to coming to your country had I begun to explore and understand issues of systemic racism and oppression. Leveraging my background as an instructor for Outward Bound in the United States, I spent the next year facilitating interracial teambuilding Outward Bound courses in Lesotho for South African employees of mining companies, banks, and pharmaceuticals.

Having just learned of my own unconscious racism from growing up in the United States, it was a healing experience to facilitate such a powerful coming together of different races in

South Africa. Each course was eight days long and included rock climbing and a wilderness hiking trip. The men from the mines had worked on the same shifts but never ate at the same table, slept in the same room, or spent any social time together. At first I identified and connected with the amazing spirit of the black and colored men and women, who often would dance around the campfire and sing amazing songs. Soon, however, I realized how much I had in common with the white men on each of these courses. Individually they were great guys, even though they were part of a system demonized around the world for being the oppressors. I looked into their eyes and saw myself. It was there I realized I needed to come back to the United States and work with people like myself, other white men. Not only did I realize it but I felt compelled to, and it has since become my life's work.

Once back in the United States, I spent four years studying, researching, and completing a dissertation about how white men learn about diversity. I found we, as white men, are completely reliant on men and women of color and white women to teach us about diversity. But for others to carry the burden to educate all white men is unsustainable. Just as I completed my research, a colleague of mine, who saw the same pattern, piloted a 3.5 day residential workshop for only white men called a "White Men's Caucus on Eliminating Racism, Sexism, and Homophobia in Organizations." We've joined together with some amazing colleagues and for thirteen years now we have taught white men and others to partner fully, through our work as a consulting company called White Men as Full Diversity Partners (see wmfdp.com). We have made a deep lasting impact in the lives of white men who are leaders in many corporations in the United States. Some day I hope to visit your country again to help seed a similar movement for white men to educate other white men in South Africa.

It was astonishing to see you emerge from 27 years of prison and engage the white men who imprisoned you from a place of love. You showed that love is the most powerful approach to drive any change. Witnessing the change happening before me while in your country was like witnessing a fairy tale. And with the same approach of love, I now witness white men from all over the United States grow the awareness and heart strength to engage their white male colleagues in creating truly inclusive organizations and communities.

I want you to know that your impact lives on in ways you may never have dreamed. Many of the white men I work with say their experience engaging with other white men around diversity is life changing. One reason is that my heart carries the same thread of love that you passed on to the white men in South Africa. It is this same thread of love that spreads though me and my colleagues into the world in ways we can all only imagine.

It was several years ago when an African American woman in one of my client organizations heard me describe my journey into diversity. Later she told me how she felt it was my experience in South Africa that compelled me to work with white men. She really got me thinking over these past few years about my path. My time in South Africa was indeed pivotal in my life. It was there I felt my life's work with other white men was no longer optional. It is as a result of this reflection that I choose now to reach out to you, while you are still here to receive my message.

Thank you for how you have impacted me with your love and attracted me to witness your message and spread it through the world with my own life. Thank you also to all the wonderful people in South Africa and Lesotho whom I had the honor to work with and learn so much from.

Most Sincerely,

Michael Welp

ACKNOWLEDGMENTS

I am grateful to many people for their support in creating this book.

Foremost is my primary editor Wendy Goldman Rohm, who steered me toward writing one single coherent caucus story by combining the true stories from twenty years of caucuses. She set the bar high to write an engaging book and taught me how to move from dialogue to the thoughts in my head, and weave in outside research and insights. I never would have written this unique book without her ongoing support and challenge.

A whole team has emerged in the past six months to bring this project to completion. Bookitect editor David Moldawer advised me on what changes to make to complete the book and got me across the finish line. From BookMatters, Tanya Grove has been an excellent copy editor, and David Peattie has created a beautiful book layout. Alan Hebel, from the Book Designers, worked with me to follow my tastes and design an enticing book cover. I appreciate the wisdom of Tim Grahl, who has coached me on the book launch process, helped me title the book, and addressed a wide mix of author questions. His online courses were also valuable. Since this fall, Jennifer Ott has aided me in countless ways as my personal assistant. I feel lucky to have such an amazing team of resourceful people.

This book would not have happened if Bill Proudman had not invited me to join him and his Inclusivity business partner Zeke Zeliff in offering the first White Men's Caucuses starting in 1997. Zeke passed away a number of years ago, and I am grateful for his enthusiasm and nonstop marketing efforts. Tim McNichol was also there from the start and, early on, became a facilitator of the caucus. Our team of caucus facilitators has expanded over the years. Mark Chesler and Michael Brazzel were subjects in my dissertation and joined our efforts. Rick Schroder, now an associate, was originally our internal client contact at Shell and participated in the caucus that took place at the Chain O' Lakes location where this book's story takes place. He remembers Snappy well and was good at spotting alligators. Over the years our caucus staff has grown, with Jim Morris, Steve Proudman, and, more recently, Noah Prince, Bo Razak, and Ethan Kerr.

Alongside this cadre of white guys are important colleagues like my WMFDP cofounder Jo Ann Morris, who has always been there to love me and spur my growth. Many more WMFDP associates have contributed to my ability to grow diversity partnerships. They include Nancy Brown, Cherie Buckner-Webb, Mary Marino, Kristin Chung-mei Lensen, Donna Ginn, Robin Gerald, Moe Carrick, Amalia Alarcon Morris, Cliff Jones, Jackie Bearce, Michael Collins,

Peggy Nagae, Emily Joye McGaughy, and Chad Simmons. I am fortunate to continue my diversity learning journey with such a rich community of WMFDP associates. Dev Pathik introduced me to my editor Wendy, and he has been a business development mentor to Bill and me for many years. Others working in our WMFDP office have made it possible to hold more than 125 White Men's Caucuses and many other labs and summits: Tim Braun (who was in the first caucus in 1997), Cynthia Nielsen, Henry Moreno, Lizette Santiago, Robin Mullins, and our longest serving office staff member, Merrilee Bruce. Pam Shelly (our controller and also Bill's wife) has been a close colleague and awesome friend to me.

I am deeply indebted to our many clients over the years, with whom I have learned so much. There are way too many of you to list here. A special thanks to Catalyst who has partnered with us since 2007, initially on research and more recently on MARC. I particularly want to thank Catalyst staff members Jeanine Prime, Jeff Barth, Heather Foust-Cummings, Sarah Dinolfo, and Elizabeth Salib. Special thanks to our Catalyst research partners Joan Buccigrossi and everyone at Rockwell Automation.

Associates Mark Chesler, Nancy Brown, Tim McNichol, and Emily Joye McGaughy provided valuable feedback, as did Elena Feliz, Lisa Kepinski, Chris DiNunzio, Marty Wolins, Ben Wolins, and Tom Gilboy. My Outward Bound friend, Joey Kenig, gave me helpful responses to drafts and suggested some funny book titles. My ex-wife, Kim Marshall, offered great feedback on initial versions of the 12 Radical Habits, and, long before that, was the main editor on my dissertation. I also benefited from a week at the Integral Center's Incubator Program in Boulder, Colorado, during the early stages of outlining my book. More recently, Frank McCloskey, Rick Stulen, and Marty Wolins helped me choose the book title and cover design.

I would like to thank two of my late Fielding University mentors who supported my journey: Len Hirsch taught me the politics of organizational change and believed in me. Charlie Seashore mentored me at both American University/NTL and Fielding, and explored with me the pathways for white men. My experience as an instructor at Voyageur Outward Bound School and Lesotho Outward Bound enabled me to facilitate complex experiential group learning. Elena Feliz and others in my American University/ NTL Masters Cohort helped me discover my many blind spots around diversity issues.

Fourteen years ago Steve Piersanti, founder of Berrett-Koehler publishing, gave me valuable coaching on an earlier book proposal, as well as encouragement on this draft.

Decker Cunov, Robert MacNaughton, Shana James, and many others at the Integral Center in Boulder have been important colleagues in deepening my skills in the arena of authentic relating and Circling.

I am thankful for the eleven years of my men's group in Sandpoint, Idaho, and especially to our group's founder, Owen Marcus, my friend Wayne Pignolet, David Barth, Brad Golphenee, Thomas Jenkins, Curtis Foster, Chris Blair, Robert Myer, David Mabelle, Tim Corcoran, and many others. Also in Sandpoint, my coach for three years, Leslie Villelli, taught me to be even happier and continues to be a great support for my daughters. Writing these acknowledgments has me feeling grateful for all the support I have and I thank all those whom I have not mentioned specifically here. My early experiences around gender came from growing up with five older sisters. I am lucky to have great siblings, as well as to have had caring parents. I am most indebted to my daughters. Lydia and Nina, you have deepened my heart and given me the opportunity to be in the most important role of my life—a Dad. Watching each of you grow is my greatest satisfaction in life. I am also thrilled to share my journey with my new life-partner, Cindy McCall, who inspires me with her own journey and playful friendship.

NOTES

INTRODUCTION

p. 1 "There's a price to be paid" Level Playing Field Institute, *Corporate Leavers Survey,* January 7, 2007. http://www.lpfi .org/corporate-leavers-survey/; Crosby Burns, *The Costly Business of Discrimination,* Center for American Progress, March 22, 2012. https://www.americanprogress.org/ issues/lgbt/report/2012/03/22/11234/the-costly-business-of -discrimination/.

p. 1 "Replacing an hourly worker" G. Robinson and K. Dechant, "Building a Business Case for Diversity," *Academy of Management Perspectives* 11, no. 3 (August 1, 1997): 21–31. doi:10.5465/ame.1997.9709231661.

p. 1 "Recent studies show one in four" Gary Langer, "One in Four U.S. Women Reports Workplace Harassment." ABC News, November 16, 2011. http://abcnews.go.com/blogs/ politics/2011/11/one-in-four-u-s-women-reports-workplace -harassment/.

p. 1 "Fully 42 percent of gay individuals" Burns, *Costly Business of Discrimination.*

p. 2 "In 2010, the top ten private plaintiff" Burns, *Costly Business of Discrimination.*

p. 2 "A study titled *The Business Case for Racial Equity*" Ani Turner, *The Business Case for Racial Equity,* W.K. Kellogg Foundation, 2013. http://www.wkkf.org/resource-directory/

resource/2013/10/the-business-case-for-racial-equity;
Donnell Alexander, "Racism Literally Costs America $2
Trillion . . . Ready to Stop Payment?" December 13, 2013.
http://www.takepart.com/article/2013/12/13/racism-literally
-costs-america-too-much-continue.

p. 2   "For example, employees are 3.5 times"   Sylvia Ann
Hewlett, Melinda Marshall, and Laura Sherbin, "How
Diversity Can Drive Innovation," *Innovation,* December
1, 2013. https://hbr.org/2013/12/how-diversity-can-drive
-innovation.

p. 2   "Hispanic purchasing power"   Matt Weeks, "Minorities
Energize U.S. Consumer Market according to UGA
Multicultural Economy Report," *UGA Today.* September
30, 2014. http://news.uga.edu/releases/article/multicultural
-economy-report-2014/.

p. 2   "The LGBT community" Human Rights Campaign,
"LGBT Marketing and Advertising" (Web page), 2015. http://
www.hrc.org/resources/lgbt-marketing-and-advertising.

p. 2   "Women represent"   Ruthie Ackerman, "Clients from
Venus," *Wall Street Journal,* April 30, 2012. http://www.wsj
.com/articles/SB10001424052970204190504577040402069714
264.

p. 2   "Recent research reveals enormous"   Cheryl Staats,
State of the Science: Implicit Bias Review 2014. Kirwan
Institute, 2014. http://kirwaninstitute.osu.edu/wp-content/
uploads/2014/03/2014-implicit-bias.pdf.

p. 3   "For example, 88 percent of whites"   Maia Szalavitz,
"The Authentic Self: How Do You Know If You're "Really"
Racist or Sexist?" | *TIME.com.* October 11, 2010. http://
healthland.time.com/2010/10/11/seeking-the-authentic-self
-how-do-you-know-if-youre-really-racist-or-sexist/.

p. 3   "In one experiment, a résumé"   Staats, *State of the Science.*

p. 3   "Other research shows that a black"   Abigail Kessler, "A
Black College Student Has the Same Chances of Getting a
Job as a White High School Dropout," June 25, 2014. http://

thinkprogress.org/education/2014/06/25/3452887/education
-race-gap/; J.B. Tucker, "The Ultimate White Privilege
Statistics & Data Post," February 28, 2015. http://www.jbw
tucker.com/ultimate-white-privilege-statistics/.

p. 3   "Meanwhile, a white male"   Devah Pager, Bruce Western,
and Bart Bonikowski, "Discrimination in a Low-Wage Labor
Market: A Field Experiment," *American Sociological Review*
74.5 (2009): 777–799.

p. 3   "Women are almost four times"   Women in the
Workplace 2015, *Corporate America Is Not on a Path to Gender
Equity.* http://womenintheworkplace.com.

p. 3   "Women in the United States"   Judith Warner, "Fact
Sheet: The Women's Leadership Gap," Center for American
Progress, March 7, 2014. https://www.americanprogress
.org/issues/women/report/2014/03/07/85457/fact-sheet-the
-womens-leadership-gap/; W. Sean Kelly and Christie Smith,
What If the Road to Inclusion Were Really an Intersection?
Deloitte University Press, December 11, 2014. http://dupress
.com/articles/multidimensional-diversity/.

p. 4   "When asked whether"   *McKinsey Quarterly,* "A CEO's
Guide to Gender Equality," (Executive briefing) November
2015. http://www.mckinsey.com/global-themes/leadership/a
-ceos-guide-to-gender-equality.

p. 4   "A new study finds"   Jonathan Woetzel, Anu Madgavkar,
Kweilin Ellingrud, Eric Labaye, Sandrine Devillard, Eric
Kutcher, James Manyika, Richard Dobbs, and Mekala
Krishnan, "How Advancing Women's Equality Can Add
$12 Trillion to Global Growth," McKinsey Global Institute,
2015. http://www.mckinsey.com/global-themes/employment
-and-growth/how-advancing-womens-equality-can-add-12
-trillion-to-global-growth.

p. 5   "Melissa Korn summarized"   Melissa Korn, "A Little
Diversity Training Goes a Long Way," *Wall Street Journal,*
July 18, 2012. http://blogs.wsj.com/atwork/2012/07/18/a-little
-diversity-training-goes-a-long-way.

p. 7 "One specific finding" Jeanine Prime, Heather Faust-Cummings, Elizabeth Salib, and Corinne A. Moss-Racusin. *Calling All White Men: Can Training Help Create Inclusive Workplaces?* Catalyst, July 18, 2012. http://www.catalyst.org/knowledge/calling-all-white-men-can-training-help-create-inclusive-workplaces.

CHAPTER ONE

p. 11 "send a fax to Lesotho Outward Bound" Lesotho Outward Bound started in 1975 within the independent country of Lesotho. It was a safe place located off of South Africa's apartheid soil to hold courses to facilitate interracial connection. The Outward Bound programming moved into South Africa after apartheid was dismantled. When I was there we held joint staff trainings with the new OB school just starting in South Africa. The location of Outward Bound's worldwide schools today can be seen at http://www.outwardbound.net/schools/.

p. 17 "lay out the Eight Critical Leadership Skills" While I've compiled the Twelve Radical Habits in this book, the Eight Critical Leadership Skills were originally identified by the three WMFDP cofounders—Jo Ann Morris, Bill Proudman, and me—and first published in the 2005 edition of our field guides. The leadership field guide *Eight Critical Leadership Skills Created through Effective Diversity Partnerships,* is now in its third edition.

CHAPTER TWO

p. 21 "One unique setting was particularly unforgettable" This book tells true stories from more than 125 White Men's Caucuses. For coherence and anonymity, they are woven into one story of a White Men's Caucus. The intent is to reveal the dialogue and learning that typically happens in this four-day residential learning lab.

p. 21 "arrives at Chain O' Lakes Resort" This site is now called The Retreat at Artesian Lakes. It was the site of our first internal caucus for Shell Oil in April of 2000. It was also the first caucus where all participants were from the corporate world. A passing train struck a tree, which took out the power line and, with it, our electricity an hour into our first evening.

p. 22 "and six rocking chairs were arranged" Most White Men's Caucuses have between twelve and eighteen participants. A few have had five to eight men. This story has only four men and two facilitators so the characters and their learning can more easily be followed.

CHAPTER THREE

p. 32 "what differences make a difference" I first heard this way of defining diversity from Ed Olson and Glenda Eoyang, who have been applying new science to organizational change. Glenda H. Eoyang and Edwin E. Olson, *Facilitating Organization Change: Lessons from Complexity Science* (San Francisco: Jossey-Bass, 2001).

p. 32 "three questions we all struggle with in groups" Marvin R. Weisbord, *Productive Workplaces: Organizing and Managing for Dignity, Meaning, and Community* (San Francisco: Jossey-Bass, 1991), page 305.

p. 36 "discovered three major barriers" Jeanine Prime and Corinne A. Moss-Racusin, *Engaging Men in Gender Initiatives: What Change Agents Need to Know* (Catalyst, 2009). http://www.catalyst.org/knowledge/engaging-men-gender-in itiatives-what-change-agents-need-know.

CHAPTER FIVE

p. 52 "Other research from the Center for Creative Leadership" CCL has several resources on this topic. See Michael M. Lombardo and Robert W. Eichinger, *Preventing Derailment:*

What to Do before It's Too Late (Greensboro, NC: Center for Creative Leadership, 1991).

CHAPTER SIX

p. 61 "explored by linguist and anthropologist Thomas Kochman" In addition to the books Tom has authored and coauthored, much of my learning comes from attending his companies' workshops. They are among the best sources I have ever found for understanding specific cultural differences. See http://www .kmadiversity.com.

p. 64 "research on culturally influenced perceptions" Thomas Kochman, *Black and White Styles in Conflict* (Chicago: University of Chicago Press, 1983).

p. 64 "recent brain research" Listen to this Nova podcast "The Deciding Factor" on PBS from March 1, 2010. http:// www.pbs.org/wgbh/nova/body/emotions-decisions.html; Jennifer Lerner, "Emotion and Decision Making," an online supplement to *Annual Review of Psychology 2015*, 66:33.1–33.25. http://scholar.harvard.edu/files/jenniferlerner/files/annual _review_supplemental_materials_formatted_oct_24.pdf; Michael A. Wheeler and Julianna Pillemer, "Moral Decision-Making: Reason, Emotion & Luck," *Harvard Business Review* (Case Study). https://hbr.org/product/moral-decision -making-reason-emotion-luck/an/910029-PDF-ENG.

p. 65 "African Americans follow the notion" Thomas Kochman and Jean Mavrelis, *Corporate Tribalism: White Men/White Women and Cultural Diversity at Work* (Chicago: University of Chicago Press, 2009).

CHAPTER EIGHT

p. 79 "One aspect of the" Peggy McIntosh, "White Privilege: Unpacking the Invisible Knapsack" and "Some Notes for

Facilitators," National Seed Project. http://nationalseedproject.org/white-privilege-unpacking-the-invisible-knapsack.

p. 82 "Ten Examples of White Privilege" Peggy McIntosh, "White Privilege and Male Privilege: A Personal Account of Coming to See Correspondences through Work in Women's Studies" (1988). http://www.collegeart.org/pdf/diversity/white-privilege-and-male-privilege.pdf.

p. 88 "The Harvard Negotiation Project conducted research" Douglas Stone, Bruce Patton, Sheila Heen, and Roger Fisher, *Difficult Conversations: How to Discuss What Matters Most* (New York: Penguin, 2010).

CHAPTER NINE

p. 91 "A young boy and his father" I first read this puzzle in a book called *Blindspot: Hidden Biases of Good People,* by Mahzarin R. Banaji and Anthony G. Greenwald (New York: Delacorte, 2013).

p. 93 "A recent cover of *Harvard Business Review*" November 2015.

p. 93 "For example, why is it" Malcolm Gladwell, *Blink: The Power of Thinking without Thinking* (New York: Little, Brown & Company, 2007).

p. 93 "The book *Blindspot* reveals" Banaji and Greenwald, *Blindspot.*

p. 93 "Researchers did just that" Unless otherwise noted, all the research on implicit bias in this chapter is from the 2014 or 2015 annual Kirwan Institute Implicit Bias Review reports. Cheryl Staats, Kelly Capatosto, Robin A. Wright, and Danya Contractor, "State of the Science: Implicit Bias Review 2015." http://kirwaninstitute.osu.edu/wp-content/uploads/2015/05/2015-kirwan-implicit-bias.pdf.

p. 94 "free ten-minute implicit bias test" Harvard University, Project Implicit, 2011. https://implicit.harvard.edu/implicit/.

p. 97 "It was December 20" This amazing program was

hosted by Earth Peoples United. See http://earthpeoples united.org/.

p. 98 "Our main host was Albert White Hat Sr.," For more on Albert White Hat Sr., see his book *Life's Journey—Zuya: Oral Teachings from Rosebud* (Salt Lake City: University of Utah Press, 2012).

p. 99 "As he describes to Ken Burns" Stephen Ives, *Ken Burns Presents: The West*, documentary. https://www.pbs.org/weta/ thewest/program/episodes/.

CHAPTER TEN

p. 101 "Television reporters had visited us before" KATU, "White Male Leaders (Mayor Included) Learning about Diversity at Golf Resort," July 10, 2014. http://katu.com/ news/local/white-male-leaders-mayor-included-learning -about-diversity-at-golf-resort.

CHAPTER ELEVEN

p. 117 "Knowing this about you" One of the operating agreements for the White Men's Caucus is that an individual chooses his level of participation and disclosure. In any activity or discussion, individuals are never forced to share anything they do not want to share. When men know they have a choice, they are usually very forthcoming.

CHAPTER TWELVE

p. 126 "in some cultures, such as can be found in Mexico" Samuel Roll and Marc Irwin, *The Invisible Border: Latino Culture in America* (Boston: Intercultural Press, 2008), Chapter 6; Diane Asitimbay, *What's Up, America?: A Foreigner's Guide to Understanding Americans* (San Diego, CA: Culturelink Press, 2009), Chapter 7.

CHAPTER THIRTEEN

p. 136 "He always finds three themes" Life Reimagined, "Richard Leider: The Power of Purpose," *YouTube*, September 17, 2012. https://www.youtube.com/watch?v=D6NIu_yx63k.

p. 138 "a documentary called *About Men*" Maja Bugge, http://aboutmenfilm.com; for additional background see the website of the founder of the Sandpoint Men's Group: http://owenmarcus.com.

p. 138 "A 2013 Pew Research" Kim Parker and Wendy Wang, "Modern Parenthood," Pew Research Center, March 14, 2013. http://www.pewsocialtrends.org/2013/03/14/modern-parent hood-roles-of-moms-and-dads-converge-as-they-balance-work-and-family/.

p. 140 "Research shows EQ, or emotional intelligence" Robert W. Eichinger and Michael M. Lombardo, *The 6 Qs of Leadership—A Blueprint for Enduring Success at the Top*, n.d. http://leadershipall.com/wp-content/uploads/2012/12 /The-6Qs-Of-Leadership.pdf; Daniel Goleman and Anne Fisher, "Success Secret: A High Emotional IQ Psychologist and Bestselling Author Daniel Goleman Says His Research Proves That Business Prizes Emotional Intelligence over Expertise in Its Managers," *Fortune*, October 26, 1998. http://archive.fortune.com/magazines/fortune/fortune_archive /1998/10/26/249986/index.htm.

p. 140 "The Chinese symbol" This symbol was first explained to me by consultant Edwin J. Nichols in several of his workshops. See http://ejnichols.org/about.html.

CHAPTER FOURTEEN

p. 143 "As the men" Catalyst, "The Double-Bind Dilemma for Women in Leadership: Damned If You Do, Doomed If You Don't," July 15, 2007. http://www.catalyst.org/knowledge/ double-bind-dilemma-women-leadership-damned-if-you-do -doomed-if-you-dont-o.

p. 146 "The latest research shows" Eileen Patten, "On

Equal Pay Day, Key Facts about the Gender Pay Gap," Pew Research Center, April 14, 2015. http://www.pewresearch.org/fact-tank/2015/04/14/on-equal-pay-day-everything-you-need-to-know-about-the-gender-pay-gap/.

p. 147 "But other studies show" Peggy Klaus, "Women and the Double Standard of Office Behavior," *New York Times*, January 9, 2015. http://www.nytimes.com/2010/03/07/jobs/07preoccupations.html.

p. 147 "In one study conducted" Dolly Chugh, Katherine L. Milkman, and Modupe Akinola, "Professors Are Prejudiced, Too," *New York Times Sunday Review*, January 30, 2015. http://www.nytimes.com/2014/05/11/opinion/sunday/professors-are-prejudiced-too.html?_r=0.

p. 147 "Another study sent" Scott Jaschik, "Study Offers New Evidence That Scientists Are Biased against Women," January 21, 2016. https://www.insidehighered.com/news/2012/09/21/study-offers-new-evidence-scientists-are-biased-against-women; Kenneth Chang, "Bias Persists against Women of Science, a Study Says," *New York Times*, August 25, 2014. http://www.nytimes.com/2012/09/25/science/bias-persists-against-women-of-science-a-study-says.html.

p. 148 "the latest surveys show that only 6.1 percent" Catalyst, "Statistical Overview of Women in the Workplace," January 12, 2016. http://www.catalyst.org/knowledge/statistical-overview-women-workplace.

p. 148 "When Credit Suisse examined" Credit Suisse, "The CS Gender 3000: Women in Senior Management," September 2014. https://publications.credit-suisse.com/tasks/render/file/index.cfm?fileid=8128F3C0-99BC-22E6-838E2A5B1E4366DF.

p. 148 "suggest men take more risks" Therese Huston, "Are Women Better Decision Makers?" *New York Times Sunday Review*, October 24, 2014. http://www.nytimes.com/2014/10/19/opinion/sunday/are-women-better-decision-makers.html.

p. 149 "Perhaps that is why" Albert E. Sole, Carolyn A.

Emery, Brent E. Hagel, and Barbara A. Morrongiello, "Risk Taking in Avalanche Terrain: A Study of the Human Factor Contribution," *Clinical Journal of Sport Medicine,* November 2010 20(6):445–451. doi: 10.1097/JSM.ob013e3181fcoa6d.

p. 149 "There is also evidence" Geoff Colvin, "Women Make Groups Smarter," *Fortune,* September 18, 2014. http://fortune.com/2014/09/18/women-make-groups-smarter/.

p. 150 "Norms are not created by critical events" Edgar H. Schein, *Organizational Culture and Leadership,* 4th ed. (San Francisco: Wiley, 2010), Chapter 12.

CHAPTER FIFTEEN

p. 158 "when men took action" Adam Grant, "Why So Many Men Don't Stand Up for Their Female Colleagues," *Atlantic,* April 29, 2014. http://www.theatlantic.com/business/archive/2014/04/why-men-dont-stand-up-for-women-to-lead/361231/.

CHAPTER SIXTEEN

p. 161 "Please stand if you have ever" A number of our exercises were initially derived from Paul Kivel's publications about men's work. See PaulKivel.com.

p. 166 "When I read the book" Meg Meeker, *Strong Fathers, Strong Daughters: 10 Secrets Every Father Should Know* (New York: Random House, 2007).

p. 167 "One study showed" Greg J. Duncan, Martha Hill, and Jean Yeung, "Fathers' Activities and Children's Attainments," IPR working papers. https://ideas.repec.org/p/wop/nwuipr/96-25.html.

p. 168 "This is much more common" UN Women, "Facts and Figures: Ending Violence against Women." http://www.unwomen.org/en/what-we-do/ending-violence-against-women/facts-and-figures; World Health Organization, "Violence

against Women," January 7, 2016. http://www.who.int/media
centre/factsheets/fs239/en/.

p. 168 "nearly one in five women are raped" National Intimate
Partner and Sexual Violence Survey (NISVS), National Data
on Intimate Partner Violence, Sexual Violence, and Stalking.
http://www.cdc.gov/violenceprevention/pdf/nisvs-fact-sheet
-2014.pdf.

p. 168 "recent studies show *one in four* women" ABC News,
"One in Four U.S. Women Reports Workplace Harassment,"
November 16, 2011. http://abcnews.go.com/blogs/politics/2011
/11/one-in-four-u-s-women-reports-workplace-harassment/.

CHAPTER EIGHTEEN

p. 179 "a film by Brian McNaught" Brian McNaught,
Homophobia in the Workplace, 1993. http://www.brian-mc
naught.com/books/homophobia.htm.

CHAPTER NINETEEN

p. 190 "26 percent of transgender workers" Human Rights
Campaign. www.hrc.org.

p. 192 "Internet of cisgender privilege" Excerpted from Sam
Killermann, "30+ Examples of Cisgender Privilege," *It's
Pronounced Metrosexual*, July 6, 2012. http://itspronounced
metrosexual.com/2011/11/list-of-cisgender-privileges/.

p. 193 "69 percent of millennials favored same-sex marriage"
Public Religion Research Institute, "A Shifting Landscape:
A Decade of Change in American Attitudes about Same-Sex
Marriage and LGBT Issues," Survey, February 2014. http://
publicreligion.org/research/2014/02/2014-lgbt-survey/#.VqY3k
VMrJE5.

p. 193 "a 2013 study" Gay, Lesbian, and Straight Education
Network, "2013 National School Climate Survey." http://
www.glsen.orgv/article/2013-national-school-climate-survey.

p. 194 "An astounding 41 percent" Ann P. Haas, Philip L.

Rodgers, and Jody L. Herman, *Suicide Attempts among Transgender and Gender Non-Conforming Adults: Findings of the National Transgender Discrimination Survey*, Williams Institute, January 2014. http://williamsinstitute.law.ucla.edu /wp-content/uploads/AFSP-Williams-Suicide-Report-Final .pdf.

p. 195   "a 2014 study of millennials"   MTV Bias Survey Summary, April 2014. http://cdn.lookdifferent.org/content/ studies/000/000/001/DBR_MTV_Bias_Survey_Executive _Summary.pdf.

p. 195   "In a 2012 MTV poll"   Taylor Gordon, "Studies Reveal So-Called 'Racially Progressive' White Millennials Are Not so Different from the Racist Generations That Came before Them," *Atlanta Black Star*, January 26, 2015. http:// atlantablackstar.com/2015/01/26/studies-reveal-called-racially -progressive-white-millennials-different-racist-generations -came/.

p. 196   "75 percent of white Americans"   Christopher Ingraham, "Three Quarters of Whites Don't Have Any Non-White Friends," *Washington Post*, August 25, 2014. https:// www.washingtonpost.com/news/wonk/wp/2014/08/25/ three-quarters-of-whites-dont-have-any-non-white-friends/.

p. 196   "was a *Fortune* magazine article"   Nadira A. Hira, "You Raised Them, Now Manage Them," *Fortune*, May 28, 2007. http://connection.ebscohost.com/c/articles/25134357/you -raised-them-now-manage-them.

CHAPTER TWENTY

p. 203   "Recently I was listening to a talk by John Powell" Mariah Helgeson, "John A. Powell—Opening the Question of Race to the Question of Belonging," *On Being* (podcast), June 25, 2015. http://www.onbeing.org/program/john-a -powell-opening-the-question-of-race-to-the-question-of -belonging/7695.

CHAPTER TWENTY-TWO

p. 223 "learning a process called Circling" Bryan Bayer, *The Art of Circling*, 1st ed. (Authentic World Publishing, 2014); see also www.integralcenter.org.

p. 226 "I also led" Susan Cain, "The Power of Introverts," TED Talk, February 2012. https://www.ted.com/talks/susan _cain_the_power_of_introverts?language=en.

p. 228 "The first report" Jeanine Prime, Heather Faust-Cummings, Elizabeth Salib, and Corinne A. Moss-Racusin, *Calling All White Men: Can Training Help Create Inclusive Workplaces?* Catalyst, 2013. http://www.catalyst.org/know ledge/calling-all-white-men-can-training-help-create-in clusive-workplaces.

p. 228 "The second study" Sarah Dinolfo, Jeanine Prime, and Heather Faust-Cummings, *Anatomy of Change: How Inclusive Cultures Evolve*, Catalyst, 2013. http://www.catalyst.org/ knowledge/anatomy-change-how-inclusive-cultures-evolve.

p. 229 "researcher John Gottman" John M. Gottman, *Why Marriages Succeed or Fail: And How You Can Make Yours Last* (London: Bloomsbury, 1997); John M. Gottman and Nan Silver, *The Seven Principles for Making Marriage Work* (New York: Three Rivers Press, 2002); Emily Esfahani Smith, "Masters of Love," *Atlantic*, June 12, 2014. http://www .theatlantic.com/health/archive/2014/06/happily-ever-after /372573/.

p. 229 "when I studied Keith Johnstone's book" Keith Johnstone, *Impro: Improvisation and the Theatre*, 2nd ed. (New York: Theatre Arts Books, 1987).

BIBLIOGRAPHY

2015 Women in the Workplace Study. 2015. http://womeninthework place.com.

ABC News. "One in Four U.S. Women Reports Workplace Harassment." November 16, 2011. http://abcnews.go.com/ blogs/politics/2011/11/one-in-four-u-s-women-reports-work place-harassment/.

Ackerman, Ruthie. "Clients from Venus." *Wall Street Journal,* April 30, 2012. http://www.wsj.com/articles/SB1000142405297 0204190504577040402069714264.

Alexander, Donnell. *Racism Literally Costs America $2 Trillion . . . Ready to Stop Payment?* December 13, 2013. http://www.take part.com/article/2013/12/13/racism-literally-costs-america-too -much-continue.

Aron, A., E. Melinat, E. N. Aron, R. D. Vallone, and R. J. Bator. "The Experimental Generation of Interpersonal Closeness: A Procedure and Some Preliminary Findings." *Personality and Social Psychology Bulletin* 23, no. 4 (April 1, 1997): 363–377. doi:10.1177/0146167297234003.

Arrien, Angeles. *Working Together: Producing Synergy by Honoring Diversity.* 1st ed. Pleasanton, CA: New Leaders Press, 1998.

Asitimbay, Diane. *What's Up, America?: A Foreigner's Guide to Understanding Americans.* San Diego, CA: Culturelink Press, 2009.

Atkinson, William. "Bringing Diversity to White Men." *HR Magazine,* September 2001.

Ayres, Ian. "When Whites Get a Free Pass: Research Shows White Privilege Is Real." *New York Times,* April 16, 2015. http://www.nytimes.com/2015/02/24/opinion/research-shows -white-privilege-is-real.html.

Bayer, Bryan. *The Art of Circling.* 1st ed. Authentic World Publishing, 2014.

Bianco, Marcie. "Wharton Study Shows the Shocking Result When Women and Minorities Email Their Professors." *Mic,* May 1, 2014. http://mic.com/articles/88731/wharton-study -shows-the-shocking-result-when-women-and-minorities -email-their-professors.

Black, Michele C., Kathleen C. Basile, Matthew J. Breiding, Sharon G. Smith, Mikel L. Walters, Melissa T. Merrick, Jieru Chen, and Mark R. Stevens. "National Intimate Partner and Sexual Violence Survey." Atlanta, GA: National Center for Injury Prevention and Control Centers for Disease Control and Prevention, November 2011. http://www.cdc.gov/ violenceprevention/pdf/nisvs_executive_summary-a.pdf.

Blake, John. "When You're the Only White Person in the Room." *CNN,* September 11, 2014. http://www.cnn.com/2014 /09/11/us/white-minority/.

Block, Peter. *The Answer to How Is Yes: Acting on What Matters.* 1st ed. San Francisco: Berrett-Koehler, 2001.

Brown, C. G. "American Racial Incident Bingo." *Democratic Underground,* December 4, 2014. http://www.democratic underground.com/118710067.

Bugge, Maja. *About Men.* http://aboutmenfilm.com.

Burns, Crosby. *The Costly Business of Discrimination.* Center for American Progress. 2012. https://www.americanprogress.org /issues/lgbt/report/2012/03/22/11234/the-costly-business-of -discrimination/.

Bushe, Gervase R., and Robert J. Marshak, eds. *Dialogic Organization Development: The Theory and Practice of*

Transformational Change. San Francisco: Berrett-Koehler, 2015.

Bussey, John. "Gender Wage Gap Reflects the 'Ask' Gap." *Wall Street Journal*, October 10, 2014. http://www.wsj.com/articles/gender-wage-gap-reflects-the-ask-gap-1412980899.

Cain, Susan. *The Power of Introverts*. TED Talk. February 2012. https://www.ted.com/talks/susan_cain_the_power_of_intro verts?language=en.

Carroll, Michael. "How Empathy Paves the Way for Innovation." *Fast Company*, November 12, 2012. http://www.fastcompany.com/3002832/how-empathy-paves-way -innovation.

Cashman, Kevin. *The Pause Principle: Step Back to Lead Forward*. San Francisco: Berrett-Koehler, 2012.

Catalyst. "The Double-Bind Dilemma for Women in Leadership: Damned If You Do, Doomed If You Don't." July 15, 2007. http://www.catalyst.org/knowledge/double-bind -dilemma-women-leadership-damned-if-you-do-doomed-if -you-dont-0.

Catalyst. "Infographic: Inclusion Matters." March 2, 2015. http://www.catalyst.org/knowledge/infographic-inclusion-matters.

Catalyst. "Sex Discrimination and Sexual Harassment." May 28, 2015. http://www.catalyst.org/knowledge/sex-discrimination -and-sexual-harassment-0.

Catalyst. "Statistical Overview of Women in the Workplace." March 3, 2014. http://www.catalyst.org/knowledge/statistical -overview-women-workplace.

Catalyst. "What Is Unconscious Bias?" December 11, 2014. http: //www.catalyst.org/knowledge/what-unconscious-bias.

Catalyst. "White Men as Full Diversity Partners." September 2014. http://wmfdp.com/catalyst-infographic/.

Chang, Kenneth. "Bias Persists against Women of Science, a Study Says." *New York Times*, August 25, 2014. http://www.ny times.com/2012/09/25/science/bias-persists-against-women-of -science-a-study-says.html.

Chemaly, Soraya. "There's No Comparing Male and Female Harassment Online." *Time*, September 9, 2014. http://time .com/3305466/male-female-harassment-online/.

Chugh, Dolly, Modupe Akinola, and Katherine L. Milkman. "What Happens Before? A Field Experiment Exploring How Pay and Representation Differentially Shape Bias on the Pathway into Organizations" (Paper). December 13, 2014. http://papers.ssrn.com/sol3/papers.cfm?abstract_id=2063742.

Chugh, Dolly, Katherine L. Milkman, and Modupe Akinola. "Professors Are Prejudiced, Too." *New York Times Sunday Review*, January 30, 2015. http://www.nytimes.com/2014 /05/11/opinion/sunday/professors-are-prejudiced-too.html ?_r=0.

Cloke, Kenneth. "Bringing Oxytocin into the Room: Notes on the Neurophysiology of Conflict." International Mediation Institute. January 2009. https://imimediation.org/ oxytocin_ken_cloke.

Colvin, Geoff. "Women Make Groups Smarter." *Fortune*, September 18, 2014. http://fortune.com/2014/09/18/women -make-groups-smarter/.

Cooperrider, David. "Leadership Excellence." March 1, 2012. https://weatherhead.case.edu/executive-education/programs /leadership-deep-dive/leadership-excellence-magazine/files/ assets/basic-html/page4.html.

Cooperrider, David. "Three Circles of the Strengths Revolution." March 2012. http://www.davidcooperrider.com/wp-content/ uploads/2011/10/3-Circles-of-Strengths-Revolution-x.pdf.

Credit Suisse. "The CS Gender 3000: Women in Senior Management." September 2014. https://publications.credit -suisse.com/tasks/render/file/index.cfm?fileid=8128F3C0-99 BC-22E6-838E2A5B1E4366DF.

Davis, Kathleen. "5 Practical Things Men Can Do for Gender Equality at Work." *Fast Company*. October 21, 2014. http:// www.fastcompany.com/3037193/strong-female-lead/5-prac tical-things-men-can-do-for-gender-equality-at-work.

DBR. MTV Bias Survey Summary. April 2014. http://cdn.look
 different.org/content/studies/000/000/001/DBR_MTV_Bias
 _Survey_Executive_Summary.pdf.

Deutsch, Barry. "A Concise History of Black-White Relations
 in the United States." *Everyday Feminism*, October 8, 2014.
 http://everydayfeminism.com/2014/10/history-of-black-white
 -relations/.

Dinolfo, Sarah, Jeanine Prime, and Heather Faust-Cummings.
 Anatomy of Change: How Inclusive Cultures Evolve. Catalyst.
 2013. http://www.catalyst.org/knowledge/anatomy-change
 -how-inclusive-cultures-evolve.

Duncan, Greg J., Martha Hill, and Jean Yeung. "Fathers'
 Activities and Children's Attainments." *Ideas.* n.d. https://
 ideas.repec.org/p/wop/nwuipr/96-25.html.

Dusenbery, Maya. "Chart of the Day: How Men and Women
 Are Criticized in Performance Reviews." *Feministing.* 2015.
 http://feministing.com/2014/09/02/chart-of-the-day-how
 -men-and-women-are-criticized-in-performance-reviews/.

Eichinger, Robert W., and Michael M. Lombardo. *The 6 Qs of
 Leadership—A Blueprint for Enduring Success at the Top.* 2004.
 http://leadershipall.com/wp-content/uploads/2012/12/The
 -6Qs-Of-Leadership.pdf.

El-Erian, Mohamed. "Father and Daughter Reunion." *Worth.*
 August 21, 2015. http://www.worth.com/articles/father-and
 -daughter-reunion/.

Freedman, Jill, and Gene Combs. *Narrative Therapy: The Social
 Construction of Preferred Realities.* New York: W. W. Norton
 & Company, 1996.

Fulwiler, Michael. "The 6 Things That Predict Divorce."
 Gottman Institute. October 10, 2014. http://www.gottman
 blog.com/archives/2014/10/31/the-6-things-that-predict
 -divorce.

Gay, Lesbian & Straight Education Network. "2013 National
 School Climate Survey." http://www.glsen.org/article/2013
 -national-school-climate-survey.

Gino, Francesca. "Ending Gender Discrimination Requires More Than a Training Program." *Harvard Business Review*, October 10, 2014. https://hbr.org/2014/10/ending-gender -discrimination-requires-more-than-a-training-program.

Gladwell, Malcolm. *Blink: The Power of Thinking without Thinking*. 1st ed. New York: Little, Brown & Company, 2007.

Goldberg, Denis. *A Life for Freedom: The Mission to End Racial Injustice in South Africa*. Lexington, KY: University Press of Kentucky, 2016.

Goleman, Daniel, and Anne Fisher. "Success Secret: A High Emotional IQ Psychologist and Bestselling Author Daniel Goleman Says His Research Proves That Business Prizes Emotional Intelligence over Expertise in Its Managers." *Fortune*, October 26, 1998. http://archive.fortune.com/maga zines/fortune/fortune_archive/1998/10/26/249986/index.htm.

Gordon, Taylor. "Studies Reveal So-Called 'Racially Progressive' White Millennials Are Not so Different from the Racist Generations That Came before Them." *Atlanta Black Star*, January 26, 2015. http://atlantablackstar.com/2015/01/26/ studies-reveal-called-racially-progressive-white-millennials -different-racist-generations-came/.

Gottman, John M. *Why Marriages Succeed or Fail: And How You Can Make Yours Last*. London: Bloomsbury, 1997.

Gottman, John M., and Julie Gottman. "How to Keep Love Going Strong." *Yes*. January 26, 2015. http://www.yesmagazine .org/issues/what-happy-families-know/how-to-keep-love -going-strong.

Gottman, John M., and Nan Silver. *The Seven Principles for Making Marriage Work*. New York: Three Rivers Press, 2002.

Grant, Adam. "Why So Many Men Don't Stand Up for Their Female Colleagues." *Atlantic*, April 29, 2014. http://www. theatlantic.com/business/archive/2014/04/why-men-dont- stand-up-for-women-to-lead/361231/.

Greenwald, Anthony G., and Mahzarin Banjo. *Blindspot: Hidden Biases of Good People*. New York: Delacorte Press, 2013.

Haas, Ann P., Philip L. Rodgers, and Jody L. Herman. *Suicide Attempts among Transgender and Gender Non-Conforming Adults: Findings of the National Transgender Discrimination Survey.* The Williams Institute. 2014. http://williamsinstitute .law.ucla.edu/wp-content/uploads/AFSP-Williams-Suicide -Report-Final.pdf.

Hall, Edward T. *Beyond Culture.* 1st ed. New York: Anchor Press, 1976.

Hallett, Stephanie. "Startling Stats on Transgender Discrimination." *Ms. Magazine,* February 7, 2011. http://ms magazine.com/blog/2011/02/07/startling-stats-on-transgender -discrimination/.

Hallett, Stephanie. "25 Facts about Rape in America." *Ms. Magazine,* May 2, 2011. http://msmagazine.com/blog/2011/05 /02/25-facts-about-rape-in-america/.

Harvard University. Project Implicit. 2011. https://implicit .harvard.edu/implicit/.

Hegewisch, Ariane, and Heidi Hartmann. "The Gender Wage Gap: 2014." Institute for Women's Policy Research. September 2015. http://www.iwpr.org/publications/pubs/the -gender-wage-gap-2014.

Helgeson, Mariah. "John A. Powell—Opening the Question of Race to the Question of Belonging." *On Being* (podcast), June 25, 2015. http://www.onbeing.org/program/john-a -powell-opening-the-question-of-race-to-the-question-of -belonging/7695.

Hewlett, Sylvia Ann, Melinda Marshall, and Laura Sherbin. "How Diversity Can Drive Innovation." Innovation. December 1, 2013. https://hbr.org/2013/12/how-diversity-can-drive -innovation.

Hill, Catherine. "The Simple Truth about the Gender Pay Gap (Fall 2015)." American Association of University Women. http://www.aauw.org/resource/the-simple-truth -about-the-gender-pay-gap/.

Hira, Nadira A. "You Raised Them, Now Manage Them."

Fortune, May 28, 2007. http://connection.ebscohost.com/c/
articles/25134357/you-raised-them-now-manage-them.

Hofstede, Geert H. *Cultures and Organizations: Software of
the Mind—Intercultural Cooperation and Its Importance for
Survival*. New York: McGraw-Hill, 1991.

Human Rights Campaign. "LGBT Marketing and Advertising."
2015. http://www.hrc.org/resources/lgbt-marketing-and
-advertising.

Huston, Therese. "Are Women Better Decision Makers?" *New
York Times Sunday Review*, October 24, 2014. http://www
.nytimes.com/2014/10/19/opinion/sunday/are-women-better
-decision-makers.html.

Ibarra, Herminia. "The Authenticity Paradox." *Harvard Business
Review*, January 1, 2015. https://hbr.org/2015/01/the-authen
ticity-paradox.

Ingraham, Christopher. "Three Quarters of Whites Don't Have
Any Non-White Friends." *Washington Post*, August 25, 2014.
https://www.washingtonpost.com/news/wonk/wp/2014/08/25
/three-quarters-of-whites-dont-have-any-non-white-friends/.

Ipsaro, Anthony J. *White Men, Women & Minorities in the
Changing Work Force*. Denver, CO: Meridian Associates, 1997.

Ives, Stephen. *Ken Burns Presents: The West*. Documentary.
https://www.pbs.org/weta/thewest/program/episodes/.

Jaschik, Scott. "Explaining the Gender Gap in Pay." *Inside
Higher Ed*, December 10, 2015. https://www.insidehighered
.com/news/2006/04/13/gender.

Jaschik, Scott. "Smoking Gun on Sexism?" *Inside Higher Ed*,
September 21, 2012. https://www.insidehighered.com/
news/2012/09/21/study-offers-new-evidence-scientists-are
-biased-against-women.

Jaschik, Scott. "Study Finds That Faculty Members Are More
Likely to Respond to White Males than Others." *Inside
Higher Ed*, October 20, 2015. https://www.insidehighered
.com/news/2014/04/24/study-finds-faculty-members-are
-more-likely-respond-white-males-others.

Jenkins, Alan. *Invitations to Responsibility: The Therapeutic Engagement of Men Who Are Violent and Abusive.* 3rd ed. Adelaide, South Australia: Dulwich Centre Publications, 1990.

Johnson, Barry. *Polarity Management: Identifying and Managing Unsolvable Problems.* Amherst, MA: Human Resource Development Press, 1996.

Johnstone, Keith. *Impro: Improvisation and the Theatre.* 2nd ed. New York: Theatre Arts Books, 1987.

Kaplan, Robert, and Robert Kaiser. *Fear Your Strengths: What You Are Best at Could Be Your Biggest Problem.* San Francisco: Berrett-Koehler Publishers, 2013.

KATU. "White Male Leaders (Mayor Included) Learning about Diversity at Golf Resort." July 10, 2014. Posted December 10, 2015. http://katu.com/news/local/white-male-leaders-mayor-included-learning-about-diversity-at-golf-resort.

Kelly, W. Sean, and Christie Smith. *What If the Road to Inclusion Were Really an Intersection?* Lexington, KY: Deloitte University Press, 2014. http://dupress.com/articles/multidimensional-diversity/.

Kessler, Abigail. *A Black College Student Has the Same Chances of Getting a Job as a White High School Dropout.* June 25, 2014. http://thinkprogress.org/education/2014/06/25/3452887/education-race-gap/.

Kilbourne, Jean. *Killing Us Softly 4.* 2010. http://www.mediaed.org/cgibin/commerce.cgi?preadd=action&key=241.

Killermann, Sam. "30+ Examples of Cisgender Privilege." *It's Pronounced Metrosexual.* 2014. http://itspronouncedmetrosexual.com/2011/11/list-of-cisgender-privileges/.

Kimmel, Michael. "Fired for Being Beautiful." *New York Times,* August 12, 2014. http://www.nytimes.com/2013/07/17/opinion/fired-for-being-beautiful.html.

Klaus, Peggy. "Women and the Double Standard of Office Behavior." *New York Times,* January 9, 2015. http://www.nytimes.com/2010/03/07/jobs/07preoccupations.html.

Kochman, Thomas. *Black and White Styles in Conflict*. Chicago: University of Chicago Press, 1983.

Kochman, Thomas, and Jean Mavrelis. *Corporate Tribalism: White Men/White Women and Cultural Diversity at Work*. 1st Edition. Chicago: University of Chicago Press, 2009.

Korn, Melissa. "A Little Diversity Training Goes a Long Way." *Wall Street Journal*, July 18, 2012. http://blogs.wsj.com/atwork/2012/07/18/a-little-diversity-training-goes-a-long-way.

Langer, Gary. "One in Four U.S. Women Reports Workplace Harassment." ABC News, November 16, 2011. http://abcnews.go.com/blogs/politics/2011/11/one-in-four-u-s-women-reports-workplace-harassment/.

Lerner, J. S. "Emotion and Decision Making." Online Supplement of *Annual Review of Psychology* 2015. 66:33.1–33.25. http://scholar.harvard.edu/files/jenniferlerner/files/annual_review_supplemental_materials_formatted_oct_24.pdf.

Level Playing Field Institute. Corporate Leavers. 2007. http://www.lpfi.org/corporate-leavers-survey/.

Levin, David. "The Deciding Factor." Episode of PBS podcast NOVA. March 1, 2010. http://www.pbs.org/wgbh/nova/body/emotions-decisions.html.

Lien, Tracey. "Why Are Women Leaving the Tech Industry in Droves?" *Los Angeles Times*, February 22, 2015. http://www.latimes.com/business/la-fi-women-tech-20150222-story.html.

Life Reimagined. "Richard Leider: The Power of Purpose." *YouTube*. September 17, 2012. https://www.youtube.com/watch?v=D6NIu_yx63k.

Lindner, Emilee. "19 Facts That Will Make You Think Differently about Race." MTV News, April 30, 2014. http://www.mtv.com/news/1817702/19-facts-that-will-make-you-think-differently-about-race/.

Lipman, Joanne. "Women at Work: A Guide for Men." *Wall Street Journal*. December 12, 2014. http://www.wsj.com/articles/women-at-work-a-guide-for-men-1418418595.

Lloyd Fickett & Associates, Inc. "Collaborative Leadership

Moves." 2009. http://www.collaborativeway.com/wp-content/uploads/2015/08/collaborative-leadership-moves.pdf.

Lombardo, Michael M., and Robert W. Eichinger. *Preventing Derailment: What to Do before It's Too Late.* Greensboro, NC: Center for Creative Leadership (1992 printing).

Luhby, Tami. "5 Disturbing Stats on Black-White Financial Inequality." CNN, August 21, 2014. http://money.cnn.com/2014/08/21/news/economy/black-white-inequality/.

Malone, Luke. "Transgender Suicide Attempt Rates Are Staggering." *Vocativ.* http://www.vocativ.com/culture/lgbt/transgender-suicide/.

Marcus, Owen. *Grow Up: A Man's Guide to Masculine Emotional Intelligence.* Edited by Theresa Renner. United States: New Tribe Press, 2013.

Marcus, Owen. *Masculine Emotional Intelligence.* http://owenmarcus.com.

Marshak, Robert. *Organizational Change: Views from the Edge.* The Lewin Center, 2009.

McCandless, David. "Diversity in Tech." *Information Is Beautiful.* http://www.informationisbeautiful.net/visualizations/diversity-in-tech/.

McElwee, Sean. "Opinion: Are Millennials Tolerant Racists?" *Al Jazeera America*, January 26, 2015. http://america.aljazeera.com/opinions/2015/1/are-millennials-tolerant-racists.html.

McIntosh, Peggy. "White Privilege: Unpacking the Invisible Knapsack" and "Some Notes for Facilitators." National Seed Project. http://nationalseedproject.org/white-privilege-unpacking-the-invisible-knapsack.

McIntosh, Peggy. "White Privilege and Male Privilege: A Personal Account of Coming to See Correspondences through Work in Women's Studies." 1988. http://www.collegeart.org/pdf/diversity/white-privilege-and-male-privilege.pdf.

McKinsey Quarterly. "A CEO's Guide to Gender Equality." (Executive briefing) November 2015. http://www.mckinsey

.com/global-themes/leadership/a-ceos-guide-to-gender
-equality.

McNaught, Brian. *Homophobia in the Workplace.* 1993. http://
www.brianmcnaught.com/books/homophobia.htm.

Meeker, Meg. *Strong Fathers, Strong Daughters: 10 Secrets Every
Father Should Know.* New York: Random House, 2007.

Mercer. "When Women Thrive, Businesses Thrive." 2014. http://
www.mercer.com/content/dam/mercer/attachments/global
/Talent/gender-diversity/Gender-Diversity-When-women
-thrive-businesses-thrive-Mercer.pdf.

Miller, Frederick A., and Judith H. Katz. *The Inclusion Breakthrough: Unleashing the Real Power of Diversity.* 1st ed. San
Francisco: Berrett-Koehler Publishers, 2002.

Mindell, Arnold. *Sitting in the Fire: Large Group Transformation
Using Conflict and Diversity.* 1st ed. Portland, OR: Lao Tse
Press, 1995.

Mohammed, Amina. "Why Inequality Is 2015's Most Worrying
Trend." *World Economic Forum.* November 7, 2014. https://
agenda.weforum.org/2014/11/inequality-2015s-worrying
-trend/.

"Moral Decision-Making: Reason, Emotion & Luck." *Harvard
Business Review* (Case Study). https://hbr.org/product/moral
-decision-making-reason-emotion-luck/an/910029-PDF
-ENG.

Morris, Jo Ann, Bill Proudman, and Michael Welp. *Diversity
Partnership Tips for White Women and People of Color to Engage
White Men.* Portland, OR: White Men as Full Diversity
Partners, 2005.

Moss-Racusin, Corinne A., John F. Dovidio, Victoria L.
Brescoll, Mark J. Graham, and Jo Handelsman. "Science
Faculty's Subtle Gender Biases Favor Male Students."
Proceedings of the National Academy of Sciences 109, no. 41
(October 9, 2012): 16474–16479. doi:10.1073/pnas.1211286109.
http://www.pnas.org/content/109/41/16474.full.

Napier, Rodney W., and Matti K. Gershenfeld. *Making Groups*

Work: A Guide for Group Leaders. Boston: Houghton Mifflin, 1983.

National Intimate Partner and Sexual Violence Survey (NISVS), National Data on Intimate Partner Violence, Sexual Violence, and Stalking. 2014. http://www.cdc.gov/violenceprevention/pdf/nisvs-fact-sheet-2014.pdf.

Nazar, Jason. "35 Questions That Will Change Your Life." *Forbes*, September 5, 2013. http://www.forbes.com/sites/jason nazar/2013/09/05/35-questions-that-will-change-your-life/.

Nevis, Edwin C. *Organizational Consulting: A Gestalt Approach.* Cambridge, MA: Analytic Press, 1987.

Nevis, Edwin C., Joan E. Lancourt, and Helen C. Vassallo. *Intentional Revolutions: A Seven-Point Strategy for Transforming Organizations.* 1st ed. San Francisco: Jossey-Bass, 1996.

New York Times Sunday Review. "Silicon Valley's Diversity Problem." October 9, 2014. http://www.nytimes.com/2014/10/05/opinion/sunday/silicon-valleys-diversity-problem.html?_r=0.

Newsom, Jennifer Siebel. *Miss Representation.* Representation Project, 2011. http://therepresentationproject.org/film/miss-representation/.

Olson, Edwin E., and Glenda H. Eoyang. *Facilitating Organization Change: Lessons from Complexity Science.* 1st ed. San Francisco: Jossey-Bass, 2001.

Oudekerk, Barbara, Dara Blackman-Demner, and Carrie Mulford. "Teen Dating Violence." U.S. Department of Justice. November 2014. https://www.ncjrs.gov/pdffiles1/nij/248337.pdf.

Pager, Devah, Bruce Western, and Bart Bonikowski. "Discrimination in a Low-Wage Labor Market: A Field Experiment." *American Sociological Review* 74.5 (2009): 777–799.

Palmer, Parker J. *Healing the Heart of Democracy: The Courage to Create a Politics Worthy of the Human Spirit*. 1st ed. San Francisco, CA: Wiley, 2011.

Parker, Kim, and Wendy Wang. "Modern Parenthood." March 14, 2013. http://www.pewsocialtrends.org/2013/03/14/modern -parenthood-roles-of-moms-and-dads-converge-as-they -balance-work-and-family/.

Parker, Palmer. "Five Habits to Heal the Heart of Democracy." http://www.globalonenessproject.org/library/articles/five -habits-heal-heart-democracy.

Patten, Eileen. "On Equal Pay Day, Key Facts about the Gender Pay Gap." Pew Research Center. April 14, 2015. http://www .pewresearch.org/fact-tank/2015/04/14/on-equal-pay-day -everything-you-need-to-know-about-the-gender-pay-gap/.

Prime, Jeanine, Heather Faust-Cummings, Elizabeth Salib, and Corinne A. Moss-Racusin. *Calling All White Men: Can Training Help Create Inclusive Workplaces?* Catalyst, July 18, 2012. http://www.catalyst.org/knowledge/calling-all-white -men-can-training-help-create-inclusive-workplaces.

Prime, Jeanine, and Corinne A. Moss-Racusin. *Engaging Men in Gender Initiatives: What Change Agents Need to Know.* Catalyst, May 4, 2009. http://www.catalyst.org/knowledge/ engaging-men-gender-initiatives-what-change-agents-need -know.

Prime, Jeanine, and Elizabeth Salib. "Infographic: Inclusion Matters." *Catalyst*, March 2, 2015. http://www.catalyst.org/ knowledge/infographic-inclusion-matters.

Prime, Jeanine, and Elizabeth Salib. "The Best Leaders Are Humble Leaders." May 12, 2014. https://hbr.org/2014/05/the -best-leaders-are-humble-leaders.

Proudman, Bill. "How to Make White Males Understand." April 24, 2012. http://www.diversityjournal.com/10211-how-to -make-white-males-understand/.

Proudman, Bill, Michael Welp, and Jo Ann Morris. *Diversity Partnership Tips for White Men.* Portland, OR: White Men as Full Diversity Partners, 2005.

Public Religion Research Institute. "A Shifting Landscape: A Decade of Change in American Attitudes about Same-Sex Marriage and LGBT Issues." Survey. February 2014. http://publicreligion.org/research/2014/02/2014-lgbt-survey/#.VqY3k VMrJE5.

Rape, Abuse & Incest National Network (RAINN). Statistics page. https://rainn.org/statistics.

Robinson, G., and K. Dechant. "Building a Business Case for Diversity." *Academy of Management Perspectives* 11, no. 3 (August 1, 1997): 21–31. doi:10.5465/ame.1997.9709231661.

Roll, Samuel, and Marc Irwin. *The Invisible Border: Latino Culture in America.* Boston: Intercultural Press, 2008.

Ross, Howard J. *Everyday Bias: Identifying and Navigating Unconscious Judgments in Our Daily Lives.* Lanham, MD: Rowman & Littlefield Publishers, 2014.

Rothman, Joshua. "The Origins of 'Privilege.'" May 12, 2014. http://www.newyorker.com/books/page-turner/the-origins -of-privilege.

Rudolph, Dana. "Peggy McIntosh's White Privilege Papers." http://nationalseedproject.org/peggy-mcintosh-s-white -privilege-papers.

Sandberg, Sheryl, and Adam Grant. "How Men Can Succeed in the Boardroom and the Bedroom." *New York Times Sunday Review*, March 16, 2015. http://www.nytimes.com/2015/03/08 /opinion/sunday/sheryl-sandberg-adam-grant-how-men-can -succeed-in-the-boardroom-and-the-bedroom.html.

Sangweni, Yolanda. "Unwritten Rules for Women in the Work-place." *Essence*, February 4, 2010. http://www.essence.com /2010/02/05/unwritten-rules-for-women-in-the-workpla.

Schaefer, Emmett, and James W. Loewen. *White Men Challenging Racism: 35 Personal Stories.* Edited by Cooper Thompson, Emmett Schaeffer, and Harry Brod. Durham, NC: Duke University Press Books, 2003.

Schein, Edgar H. *Humble Inquiry: The Gentle Art of Asking Instead of Telling.* 1st ed. San Francisco: Berrett-Koehler Publishers, 2013.

Schein, Edgar H. *Organizational Culture and Leadership.* 4th ed. San Francisco: Wiley, 2010.

Shelton, Chuck. *Leadership 101 for White Men: How to Work Successfully with Black Colleagues and Customers.* New York: Morgan James Publishing, 2008.

Simmons, Rachel. *Odd Girl Out: The Hidden Culture of Aggression in Girls.* 1st ed. Orlando, FL: Harcourt Brace International, 2003.

Smith, Emily Esfahani. "Masters of Love." *Atlantic,* June 12, 2014. http://www.theatlantic.com/health/archive/2014/06/happily-ever-after/372573/.

Sole, Albert E., Carolyn A. Emery, Brent E. Hagel, and Barbara A. Morrongiello. "Risk Taking in Avalanche Terrain: A Study of the Human Factor Contribution." *Clinical Journal of Sport Medicine,* November 2010 20(6):445–451. doi: 10.1097/JSM.0b013e3181fcoa6d.

Staats, Cheryl, Kelly Capatosto, Robin Wright, and Danya Contractor. *State of the Science: Implicit Bias Review 2014.* Kirwan Institue, 2014. http://kirwaninstitute.osu.edu/wp-content/uploads/2014/03/2014-implicit-bias.pdf.

Stampler, Laura. "CEO Dads Open Up about Balancing Fatherhood and Work." *Time,* September 15, 2014. http://time.com/3342431/work-life-balance-fatherhood-ceos/.

Stone, Douglas, Bruce Patton, Sheila Heen, and Roger Fisher. *Difficult Conversations: How to Discuss What Matters Most.* 10th ed. New York: Penguin (Non-Classics), 2010.

Stop Street Harassment (SSH). "Unsafe and Harassed in Public Spaces: A National Street Harassment Report." June 3, 2014. http://www.stopstreetharassment.org/wp-content/uploads/2012/08/2014-National-SSH-Street-Harassment-Report.pdf.

Swim, Janet K., and Julia C. Becker. "Seeing the Unseen." *Psychology of Women Quarterly* 35, no. 2 (June 2011): 227–242.

doi:10.1177/0361684310397509. http://pwq.sagepub.com/content
/35/2/227.abstract.

Szalavitz, Maia. "The Authentic Self: How Do You Know If
You're 'Really' Racist or Sexist?" TIME.com. October 11,
2010. http://healthland.time.com/2010/10/11/seeking-the
-authentic-self-how-do-you-know-if-youre-really-racist-or
-sexist/.

Terry, Robert W. *For Whites Only.* 1st ed. Grand Rapids:
William B. Eerdmans Publishing, 1959.

Toppo, Greg. "Growing up 'Post-Racial,' Teens Suddenly Find a
World That Isn't." *USA Today,* March 18, 2015. http://www
.usatoday.com/story/news/nation/2014/12/10/teen-attitudes
-race-diversity-america/19749199/.

Tucker, J. B. W. "The Ultimate White Privilege Statistics &
Data Post." February 28, 2015. http://www.jbwtucker.com/
ultimate-white-privilege-statistics/.

Turner, Ani. *The Business Case for Racial Equity.* W. K. Kellogg
Foundation, 2013. http://www.wkkf.org/resource-directory/
resource/2013/10/the-business-case-for-racial-equity.

Turner, Jan. "Wake Up, White Guys! Bill Proudman Tackles D
& I." March 6, 2004. https://www.womenetics.com/Article
/ArtMID/2681/ArticleID/2563/bill-proudman-diversity
-partners.

UN Women. "Facts and Figures: Ending Violence against
Women." http://www.unwomen.org/en/what-we-do/ending
-violence-against-women/facts-and-figures.

Warner, Judith. "Fact Sheet: The Women's Leadership Gap."
Center for American Progress. March 7, 2014. https://www
.americanprogress.org/issues/women/report/2014/03/07/85457/
fact-sheet-the-womens-leadership-gap/.

Weaver, Gary R., and Adam Mendelson. *America's Mid-Life
Crisis: The Future of a Troubled Superpower.* Boston, MA:
Intercultural Press, 2008.

Weeks, Matt. "Minorities Energize U.S. Consumer Market
According to UGA Multicultural Economy Report." *UGA*

Today. September 30, 2014. http://news.uga.edu/releases/article/multicultural-economy-report-2014/.

Weisbord, Marvin R. *Productive Workplaces: Organizing and Managing for Dignity, Meaning, and Community.* San Francisco: Jossey-Bass, 1991.

Welp, Michael. "Pathways to Diversity for White Males." Fielding Graduate University, 1997. http://wmfdp.com/wp-content/uploads/2016/01/white-male-pathways.pdf.

Welp, Michael. "Vanilla Voices: Researching White Men's Diversity Learning Journeys." *American Behavioral Scientist* 45, no. 8 (April 2002): 1288–1296. doi:10.1177/00027642020204500 8012. http://abs.sagepub.com/content/45/8/1288.abstract.

Welp, Michael. "Treasures and Challenges of Diversity for White Males." In *Working Together: Producing Synergy by Honoring Diversity.* Edited by Angeles Arrien. San Francisco: Berrett-Koehler, 2001.

Welp, Michael. "White Men as Advocates for Diversity." *The Diversity Factor* 12 (January 1, 2004): 5–11. http://wmfdp.com/wp-content/uploads/2016/01/the-diversity-factor.pdf.

Welp, Michael, Jo Ann Morris, and Bill Proudman. *Eight Critical Leadership Skills Created Through Effective Diversity Partnerships.* 3rd Edition. Portland, OR: White Men as Full Diversity Partners, 2015.

White Hat, Albert, Sr. *Life's Journey—Zuya: Oral Teachings from Rosebud.* Salt Lake City: University of Utah Press, 2012.

WHO. "Violence against Women." Updated January, 2016. http://www.who.int/mediacentre/factsheets/fs239/en/.

Wise, Tim J. *White like Me: Reflections on Race from a Privileged Son.* Berkeley: Soft Skull Press, 2008.

Woetzel, Jonathan, Anu Madgavkar, Kweilin Ellingrud, Eric Labaye, Sandrine Devillard, Eric Kutcher, James Manyika, Richard Dobbs, and Mekala Krishnan. "How Advancing Women's Equality Can Add \$12 Trillion to Global Growth." McKinsey Global Institute, 2015. http://www.mckinsey.com/global-themes/employment-and-growth/how-advancing-womens-equality-can-add-12-trillion-to-global-growth.

INDEX

abundance, noticing, 208–9

Acquired Male Answer Syndrome, 122

action, emphasis on. *See* doing and telling; doing vs. being

affection. *See under* homophobia

age. *See* generational differences

Allies Lab, 5, 63, 96, 224

alpha male, 24, 36, 109, 227

ambiguity, 62–63

  learning to accept, 62–64, 157, 191, 205, 218

  and turbulence, leadership skill of leveraging, 65–66, 239

  See also complexity; either/or (vs. both/and) thinking; uncertainty

anger, 45–46, 61, 67, 73, 157, 158, 201–3

  in women, 67, 157

anorexia, 166

apathy, as reason for white men not engaging, 36

appreciating and acknowledging what is working well, 217. *See also* problem to solve

authentic relating, 224

authenticity, courage in sharing one's, 136

authority. *See* Acquired Male Answer Syndrome

avoidance and hunger for nurturance. *See* nurturance/nurturing exercise

being vs. doing. *See* doing vs. being

bids (requests for connection), 229

binaries. *See* either/or (vs. both/and) thinking; multiple perspectives

Black and White Styles in Conflict (Kochman), 61–62

black- vs. white-sounding names, biases in response to, 93–94

blind men and the elephant, story of the, 41–43

ABOUT THE AUTHOR

MICHAEL WELP, Ph.D., is the co-founder of White Men as Full Diversity Partners. He is known for his authenticity, his trust-building style, and his success in using diversity as a source of transformation.

In 1990, Michael spent a year in South Africa facilitating interracial team-building for more than a dozen South African corporations. In 1996, he conducted groundbreaking research on how white men learn about diversity. This research highlighted the need for new ways to engage white men, leading Michael to cofound WMFDP the following year.

For thirty years, Michael has worked extensively with leadership teams in numerous organizations to grow leadership skills, transform conflict, and develop innovative approaches to diversity and inclusion.

Michael has designed and taught graduate courses for a number of universities and is a blogger for Catalyst's Men Advocating Real Change (MARC), an online learning community for professionals committed to achieving equality in the workplace. He has also coauthored three field guides on skill-building for leadership and diversity partnerships.

Earlier in his career, Michael learned to design and facilitate experiential learning as an Outward Bound instructor while leading canoeing, backpacking, and dogsledding expeditions. Today he lives in the mountainous lake town of Sandpoint, Idaho, with his two daughters.

Michael can be reached at welp@wmfdp.com.

ABOUT WHITE MEN
AS FULL DIVERSITY
PARTNERS

THE WMFDP WAY:
PATHWAYS TO FULL INCLUSION

White Men as Full Diversity Partners is a leadership development firm focused on inspiring courageous leaders—white men, men and women of color, and white women. We inspire leaders to examine the assumptions that influence their mindsets about leadership, partnership, and diversity. WMFDP guides leaders to a place of deeper understanding and awareness, heightened cultural competence, and transformative and courageous leadership.

We approach diversity work differently than most, if not all, consultancies. We see leadership development through a lens of inclusion and diversity. We believe that without the full engagement of white male leaders, long term change with diversity and inclusion (D&I) is not possible.

Over the last twenty years, we have established a proven track record of partnering with global organizations to change the way D&I efforts are led and practiced. We call this *The WMFDP Way*:

1. Uses a proven experiential approach that connects the heart with the head

2. Emphasizes personal transformation preceding organization change

3. Examines the role of white men and the impact of dominant business culture

4. Enables and prepares senior leaders to be courageous change agents

5. Embraces diversity as a process rather than a check-the-box solution

6. Links leadership directly with diversity and inclusion

We inspire leaders to courageously examine their assumptions, mindsets, and unconscious bias by heightening awareness about how the often invisible dimensions of difference impact communication, engagement, and partnership. As a result, leaders transform themselves and their organizations.

www.wmfdp.com

ABOUT THE WHITE MEN'S CAUCUS

The White Men's Caucus on Eliminating Racism, Sexism, and Homophobia in Organizations is a four-day residential program designed for up to eighteen white men who may attend solo or with work colleagues. Thousands of leaders have attended the White Men's Caucus since its inception in 1997, many describing the experience as life-changing.

The lab dynamics create an environment where white men can openly explore, often for the first time, their questions, confusions, hopes, and concerns related to diversity issues in their organizations and in their personal lives. The Caucus helps white men more fully see and understand their culture and privilege, and the impact of those forces on themselves and others.

This innovative white-male-only session shatters the myth that white men don't have an important role to play in creating and sustaining inclusive work environments.

FourDaysToChange.com

Visit the website FourDaysToChange.com for

- ► Latest news on the book
- ► More testimonials
- ► Discussion guides
- ► Tools & links